LINCOLN AND THE EMANCIPATION PROCLAMATION IN AMERICAN HISTORY

The IN AMERICAN HISTORY Series

In
AMERICAN
HISTORY

LINCOLN AND THE EMANCIPATION PROCLAMATION IN AMERICAN HISTORY

David M. Holford

Enslow Publishers, Inc.

40 Industrial Road   PO Box 38
Box 398   Aldershot
Berkeley Heights, NJ 07922   Hants GU12 6BP
USA   UK

http://www.enslow.com

For Betty

Library of Congress Cataloging-in-Publication Data

Holford, David M.
   Lincoln and the Emancipation Proclamation in American history / David
M. Holford.
      p. cm. — (In American history)
      Includes bibliographical references (p.) and index.
      Summary: Examines the history of the Emancipation Proclamation,
   showing its creation as a war measure designed to bring the southern states
   back to the Union and discussing its effectiveness in freeing the slaves.
      ISBN 0-7660-1456-8
      1. United States. President (1861-1865 : Lincoln). Emancipation
Proclamation—Juvenile literature. 2. Lincoln, Abraham, 1809-1865—
Juvenile literature. 3. Slaves—Emancipation—United States—Juvenile
literature. 4. United States—Politics and government—1861-1865—Juvenile
literature. [1. Emancipation Proclamation. 2. Slavery—History. 3. United
States—History—Civil War, 1861-1865.] I. Title. II. Series.
E453 .H64 2002
973.7'092—dc21

                                                                      2001004405

Printed in the United States of America

10 9 8 7 6 5 4 3 2 1

To Our Readers:
We have done our best to make sure all Internet addresses in this book were active
and appropriate when we went to press. However, the author and the publisher have
no control over and assume no liability for the material available on those Internet
sites or on other Web sites they may link to. Any comments or suggestions can be
sent by e-mail to comments@enslow.com or to the address on the back cover.

Illustration Credits: Austin History Center, Austin Public Library, p. 116;
Dictionary of American Portraits, Dover Publications, Inc., 1990, p. 91; Enslow
Publishers, Inc., pp. 45, 61, 72; Library of Congress, pp. 13, 15, 20, 23, 25, 28,
32, 35, 44, 49, 52, 56, 69, 75, 80, 103; Daguerreotype by Mathew Brady, Courtesy
of Library of Congress, taken from *Dictionary of American Portraits*, Dover
Publications, Inc., 1967, p. 64; Engraving by George E. Perine, taken from
Dictionary of American Portraits, Dover Publications, Inc., 1967, p. 82; National
Archives, pp. 11, 94, 110; National Portrait Gallery, pp. 37, 40; Courtesy New
York Historical Society, taken from *Dictionary of American Portraits*, Dover
Publications, Inc., 1967, p. 113; New York State Library, p. 16; University of Texas
libraries, pp. 88, 101.

Cover Illustrations: White House Historical Association; Library of Congress;
National Portrait Gallery; Library of Congress.

★ CONTENTS ★

It was late summer 1862. In the White House, President Abraham Lincoln was worried. An army of rebels was on the loose in western Maryland. No one in Washington, D.C., knew exactly where, but reports put the size of the force at 100,000 to 150,000 men. Among its likely destinations,

FOREVER FREE

Lincoln's advisors warned him, were Baltimore, Philadelphia, or even the nation's capital itself. Across Maryland and southern Pennsylvania, frightened citizens prepared to flee to the north.

Reacting to the threat, Lincoln sent General George McClellan and 90,000 troops to find the rebels and crush them. The president warned McClellan to keep his army between the rebel force and Washington at all times. However, the general had ignored his commander-in-chief's advice before. If the rebels somehow got past McClellan's army, they could easily capture the city. Every other day, a nervous president telegraphed the general about his progress. "How does it look now?" Lincoln anxiously asked in each telegram.[1]

A Nation Torn in Two

In 1862, the United States was embroiled in a bloody civil war, as Northerners and Southerners fought about an issue that had troubled the nation for decades. Over time, a growing number of people in the North had become critical of the South, where millions of African Americans were held as slaves. The North, with its small farms and cities full of shops and factories, had little use for slavery. Northern states had banned the practice. The South, however, had few cities and industries. Its prosperity depended on growing huge amounts of tobacco and cotton—and, white Southerners believed, on having slaves to do this work.

Over time, slaveholders became increasingly concerned about the efforts of some Northerners to prevent the spread of slavery into new territories, or to end it completely in the United States. Southerners worried about what might happen if people who opposed slavery ever gained control of the nation's government. This event, long feared in the South, came true in 1860 when Abraham Lincoln, a Republican from Illinois, was elected president of the United States.

Although Lincoln's dislike of slavery was well known, he assured Southerners that he would leave it alone where it already existed. But many Republicans in Congress were more extreme. Some of them wanted to free the slaves. With Northerners holding a majority of the seats in Congress and the Republican Lincoln about to be in the White House, some

Southerners feared passage of a national law against slavery. The only way to protect their human "property," many slaveholders believed, was to form a new nation where they would be in charge.

By the time Lincoln took office in March 1861, seven southern states had seceded, or withdrawn, from the United States and created the Confederate States of America. After fighting broke out between southern forces and the U.S. Army, four more slaveholding states seceded and joined the new nation.

Many Confederates considered themselves to be like their colonial ancestors, who had gained independence from an oppressive government in Great Britain. Lincoln and other Northerners believed that no state had the right to leave the Union. In their view, the Confederacy was not a nation, but a group of states in rebellion against the United States. When attempts to peacefully settle the dispute failed, Lincoln called on the army to force the "rebels" back into the Union.

An Important Battle

The early months of the Civil War went badly for the North. Union forces invaded Virginia three times between July 1861 and August 1862, trying to capture the Confederate capital of Richmond, Virginia, just ninety miles south of Washington, D.C. Each attempt was turned back by southern armies. Encouraged by their success, Confederate officials decided to attack the North. They believed a major victory on northern soil might put pressure on Lincoln to end the war and let the South go its own way in peace.

On September 4, 1862, a Confederate army commanded by General Robert E. Lee crossed the Potomac River into Union territory about forty miles from Washington, D.C., and disappeared into the mountains of western Maryland. While northern leaders tried not to panic, Lincoln dispatched McClellan to find the rebel army and stop it.

As his troops searched for the Southerners, McClellan had an incredible stroke of good luck. A Union soldier found a copy of Lee's invasion plans wrapped around a bunch of cigars near an abandoned Confederate camp. McClellan learned that most of Lee's army, which actually numbered only 40,000 men, was along a stream called Antietam Creek, near Sharpsburg, Maryland. The stage was set for the bloodiest day of the Civil War—the Battle of Antietam, fought on September 17, 1862.

At 6:00 A.M. McClellan ordered the attack. First, his cannons opened fire on a cornfield where Confederate troops were hiding, waiting to ambush the oncoming Union army. One of McClellan's officers described the result of the withering Union artillery fire: "Every stalk of corn in the . . . greater part of the field was cut as closely as could have been done with a knife, and the slain lay in rows, precisely as they had stood in their ranks a few moments before. It was never my misfortune to witness a more bloody, dismal battlefield."[2]

Union army supply wagons cross Antietam Creek as they head to the Battle of Antietam in September 1862.

The surviving Confederates ran for cover in a nearby woods, where they were reinforced by other parts of Lee's army. There they hid behind rocks and trees to beat back the waves of Union troops coming at them from across the blood-soaked cornfield. In one final desperate charge, more than 2,200 Union attackers were killed or wounded in just twenty minutes.[3]

Elsewhere on the battlefield, other Confederate troops took up positions along a sunken road, a deep trench worn into the earth by years of heavy wagon traffic. From this cover they poured gunfire into advancing Union forces. But each time the Northerners were hit by a Confederate volley, they reformed their lines and kept coming. Finally, the Southerners were forced to retreat. As McClellan's troops scrambled across the road in pursuit, Confederate bodies were so thick that the feet of many Union soldiers never touched the ground. When the battle ended in the late afternoon, thousands of men from both sides lay dead or dying in the fields around Antietam Creek.

"God bless you, and all with you," Lincoln had telegraphed McClellan. "Destroy the rebel army, if possible."[4] But that would not be possible this day. Lee lost over 25 percent of his force—nearly 12,000 soldiers killed or wounded. However, McClellan's losses were about the same. Both armies were too battered to fight any longer. When the Confederates began a slow retreat back into Virginia the next evening, a relieved president declared a badly needed victory for the Union army.

An Historic Announcement

Lincoln needed to label the Battle of Antietam a victory for an important reason. The president planned a drastic action that he hoped would help bring an end to the war. He had been waiting for the right time to announce this measure to the nation and the world. With the Confederates on the retreat, that time seemed to be at hand.

A Union doctor tries to care for Confederate wounded on the battlefield at Antietam. Other soldiers have set up blankets to shield the wounded men from the sun.

"I wish that we were in a better condition," Lincoln told his cabinet on the Monday following the battle. "The action of the army against the rebels has not been quite what I should have best liked. But they have been driven out of Maryland, and Pennsylvania is no longer in danger of invasion."[5] The president began to read from some handwritten pages that he had prepared. Cabinet members were not surprised at what they heard because Lincoln had told them of his plans several weeks earlier. But his historic words still must have stirred their emotions: ". . . on the first day of January in the year of our Lord, one thousand eight hundred and sixty-three, all persons held as slaves within any state, or designated part of a state, the people whereof shall then be in rebellion against the

United States shall be then, thenceforward, and forever free. . . ."[6]

These words that changed a war and a people were at the heart of the Emancipation Proclamation—an official declaration (proclamation) of freedom (emancipation) for enslaved Americans.

The president had kept his plan well-hidden. The public announcement on the evening of September 22, 1862, took the nation completely by surprise. "We shout for joy that we live to record this righteous decree," cried famous antislavery activist Frederick Douglass, himself a former slave.[7] The next day *The New York Times* declared that "no more important . . . document [was] ever issued since the foundation of this Government."[8]

Myths and Realities

The Emancipation Proclamation does indeed rank alongside the Declaration of Independence and the Constitution of the United States as one of the most important documents in American history. But it is by far the least known and most misunderstood of the three. In part, this is because myths have developed about the Emancipation Proclamation and its author that have become part of American culture.

For example, because of his action, President Lincoln is forever known as the Great Emancipator. In reality, the Emancipation Proclamation did not end slavery in the United States. In fact, it did not directly free a single slave! Furthermore, for a number of

Lincoln, seated at the left end of the table, reads his preliminary proclamation to his cabinet. The scene was recorded in this painting by Francis B. Carpenter several months later.

reasons, Lincoln was hesitant to even issue it. Just a month before making the announcement, he shared his thoughts on the subject with New York newspaper editor Horace Greeley:

> My paramount object [supreme goal] in this struggle [the Civil War] *is* to save the Union, and is *not* either to save or to destroy slavery. If I could save the Union without freeing *any* slave I would do it, and if I could save it by freeing *all* the slaves I would do it; and if I could save it by freeing some and leaving others alone I would also do that. What I do about slavery, and the colored race, I do because I believe it helps to save the Union; and what I forbear [leave alone], I forbear

SOURCE DOCUMENT

That on the first day of January in the year of our Lord, one thousand eight hundred and sixty-three, all persons held as slaves within any state, or designated part of a state, the people whereof shall then be in rebellion against the United States shall be then, thenceforward, and forever free

This passage is from the Preliminary Emancipation Proclamation that Lincoln wrote out longhand and read to his cabinet on September 22, 1862.

because I do *not* believe it would help to save the Union.[9]

In this statement can be found the real story of the Emancipation Proclamation. But to uncover this story we must first understand Lincoln and the forces that buffeted the nation during his times. Only then can we truly appreciate this great document of American history—why it was issued, what it accomplished, its limits, and why it was so long in coming.

In the decades before the Civil War, Southerners often referred to slavery as their "peculiar institution." However, they were only partly correct in their use of this term. Slavery certainly was an institution—that is, a long-established practice—in the South by the mid-1800s. But it was hardly "peculiar," or special, to that region. Slavery was well known

THE
PECULIAR
INSTITUTION

to the world. From Africa, ancient China, and India in the East, to the American Indians of the Western Hemisphere, it had been practiced around the world for thousands of years.

The First Slaves in the Americas

When Christopher Columbus returned to Spain after his voyage of discovery in 1492, he took with him a number of American Indians from the Caribbean islands he visited. These unfortunate captives remained in Europe as slaves.

The Spanish and Portuguese enslaved thousands of American Indians to do the work in their colonies in the New World. But many of these slaves died from mistreatment and from European diseases, like smallpox, to which they had no natural resistance. To solve this labor shortage, Spain and Portugal began to bring black Africans to their colonies in the early 1500s.

From the 1500s to the mid-1800s as many as eleven million people were purchased in West Africa and transported by ship across the Atlantic Ocean to the Americas. Some 400,000 to 600,000 Africans arrived between 1619 and 1808 in what is now the United States.

Africans in England's North American Colonies

In August 1619, about a year before the Pilgrims landed at Plymouth Rock, a Dutch ship sailed into Chesapeake Bay and docked at Jamestown, Virginia— England's only colony in North America at that time. On board the ship were twenty black Africans. The captain sold them to colonist John Rolfe, who needed laborers to work in his tobacco fields. Over the next thirty years, more Africans slowly arrived in the colony. By 1649 about 300 people of African birth or ancestry lived among Virginia's 15,000 white colonists. Another 750 lived in the nearby colony of Maryland, which had been founded in 1632. They accounted for less than 9 percent of that colony's population.[1]

At first, Africans in the English colonies were not enslaved. Instead they were indentured servants, people who worked without wages for several years to repay the cost of their passage to the colonies. This system provided workers that England's colonies needed as they grew. Between half and two-thirds of the Europeans who came to the colonies before the American Revolution arrived as indentured servants.

Like European indentured servants, the first Africans were freed at the end of their service period. But in the mid-1600s, some colonists stopped releasing their black indentured servants and made them into permanent slaves instead. A combination of circumstances led to this change.

In the early 1600s, slavery did not seem practical to the English colonists. Harsh conditions and disease made the death rate very high. Because the price of a slave was higher than the cost of an indentured servant, the loss was greater when a slave died. As long as enough indentured servants were available, colonists who needed workers were not willing to take the financial risks that slavery involved.

The situation began to change in the 1640s, however. A long civil war in England and other political changes reduced the flow of new colonists to America. This limited the supply of indentured labor at a time when the colonies were expanding. Farmers in Maryland and Virginia were successfully growing tobacco and putting more land into production. In addition, a colony was founded south of Virginia in 1663, from which North Carolina and South Carolina were eventually formed. This new colony also needed workers.

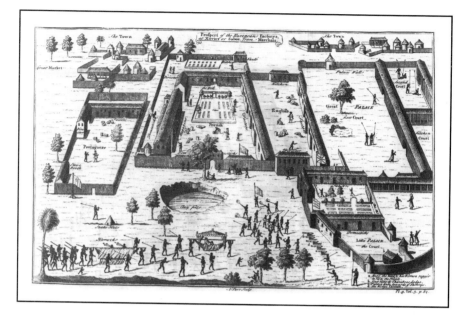

This drawing from the 1700s is of a place on Africa's west coast where European traders held Africans before shipping them off to slavery in the Americas.

Meanwhile, many former indentured servants in Virginia were unhappy because they were still poor and were not benefiting from the colony's growth and prosperity. In April 1676, about five hundred of these colonists revolted. They raided farms and burned Jamestown. Although the uprising was soon defeated, it had important consequences. Among them was that it encouraged the spread of slavery. Farmers became less willing to employ indentured servants, who might become troublemakers after they were freed. The use of slave labor did not present this problem.

In addition, by the late 1600s the death rate in the colonies had fallen, as colonists adapted to life in North

America. This reduced the financial risks of slavery. At the same time, improved conditions in England and wars in Europe made the supply of indentured servants unpredictable. But slaves and the children born to them were a dependable and continuing source of labor.

European traders were happy to supply these slaves. After 1680, Dutch slave ships began making regular calls to Viginia and Maryland. By 1710, more than 40 percent of Virginia's population—and nearly 25 percent of Maryland's—were slaves of African birth or descent.[2] In just over a century, slavery had become firmly established in England's colonies in North America.

Geography, Economics, and Slavery

When the American Revolution began in 1775, slavery existed in all of the thirteen colonies that became the United States. From the earliest times, however, the institution was more widespread in the South than it was in the North. This was due to a number of factors.

The warm climate and rich soil of the South encouraged Southerners to grow cash crops. These are crops that farmers raised not for themselves, but to sell to other people. The most important cash crop in the southern colonies was tobacco. This plant was introduced to the Europeans by American Indians, who smoked its leaves. As tobacco use became popular in Europe, colonists in Virginia, Maryland, and North Carolina planted more and more land with the crop. Great estates called plantations developed. The farmers who owned these plantations were known as planters.

Growing tobacco on a plantation required a large number of workers. African slaves, purchased with the profits from tobacco sales, gradually filled this need.

In parts of South Carolina, rice was the major cash crop. Like the growing of tobacco, the cultivation of rice required a large number of workers. Slaves were the preferred workers on rice plantations because their experience as rice farmers in West Africa provided the skills needed to grow this crop. As rice growing and the plantation system developed in South Carolina, major population shifts occurred. By 1710, the colony's nearly 5,800 slaves outnumbered the white colonists.[3]

The climate of the northern colonies—from Pennsylvania to New England—was too cold for large rice or tobacco crops. Pennsylvania, New York, and New Jersey farmers planted wheat and other grain crops, but there was little need in Europe for grain from the colonies. Therefore, the profits from farming in these colonies did not allow a plantation system to develop. Some farmers owned one or two slaves to help them in the fields. Most other slaves in the North worked as sailors or dock hands, in manufacturing, or as household servants. New York City in particular had a large slave population.

Slavery in the United States

When George Washington took the oath of office as the nation's first president in 1789, more than 80 percent of the slaves in the United States lived in four

TO BE SOLD on board the Ship *Bance-Island*, on tuesday the 6th of *May* next, at *Ashley-Ferry*; a choice cargo of about 250 fine healthy **NEGROES**, just arrived from the Windward & Rice Coast. —The utmost care has already been taken, and shall be continued, to keep them free from the least danger of being infected with the SMALL-POX, no boat having been on board, and all other communication with people from *Charles-Town* prevented.

Austin, Laurens, & Appleby.

N. B. Full one Half of the above Negroes have had the SMALL-POX in their own Country.

This newspaper ad announced the arrival and sale of a shipload of Africans by slave dealers near Charleston, South Carolina.

southern states—North Carolina, South Carolina, Maryland, and President Washington's home state of Virginia.

Across the North, with the exception of New York, slavery was in decline. Even in the South, some people thought that the region's economy might no longer be able to support the plantation system and slavery. Tobacco prices had fallen. In addition, decades of tobacco farming had exhausted the soil's richness and lowered productivity.

Some Southerners turned to growing cotton for England's textile mills—cloth-manufacturing factories that had developed during the 1700s. But it was difficult to make money growing cotton. The only variety that could survive in the United States produced a tightly woven pod of cotton fibers and seeds. Picking the seeds from only a pound of cotton took hours. This limited the amount of cotton a planter could grow and sell.

Many planters feared that neither tobacco nor cotton farming could continue to produce the income needed to support the expense of holding slaves. In 1794, President Washington warned that the situation was making slaves "a very troublesome species [type] of property."[4] In other words, he thought that slavery was becoming an economic burden on planters.

However, even as Southerners were expressing such concerns, the situation was changing. In 1793, schoolteacher Eli Whitney built a cotton gin, a wooden box with wire-fitted rollers that efficiently separated the

Cotton gins such as this one made it much easier to prepare harvested cotton for sale. This encouraged an increase in both cotton-growing and slavery.

seeds from the cotton fibers. By cranking the machine's handle, a slave could process fifty pounds of cotton in a day. The development of horse- and water-powered gins speeded the operation even more. A planter could now process all the cotton that slaves could grow.

The cotton gin's effects were immediate and remarkable. Just 6,000 bales of cotton had been produced in the South in 1792. (A bale of cotton weighs 500 pounds.) Eight years later, Southerners were producing 100,000 bales a year and the number of slaves in the South had grown by more than 200,000. But the long-term changes there were even more dramatic.

By the early 1800s, the machines that produced cloth in England had been copied in the United States. As New England developed a textile industry, planters began supplying cotton to northern factories in addition to factories in England. Southerners sought more land on which to make money by growing and selling cotton. As they pushed west, several new slave states—that is, states that allowed slavery—came into the Union.

By 1840, the South was producing more than a million bales of cotton a year, and some 2.6 million slaves lived among 4.3 million white Southerners. Over the next twenty years, both cotton and slavery continued to grow rapidly. In 1861, the year Abraham Lincoln became the nation's sixteenth president, annual cotton production reached 4 million bales. And in the seven decades since President Washington had held the office, the number of slaves in the United States had grown from fewer than 700,000 to about four million.

Southern Society and Slavery

By 1860, nearly one of every three Southerners was being held in slavery. At the same time, however, most white Southerners owned no slaves. Only 25 percent were slaveowners, and, of these, nearly three-fourths held fewer than ten slaves. Just 3 percent of slaveowners—or about seven of every thousand white

Southerners—had fifty or more slaves.[5] These were the few large, wealthy planters who from colonial times dominated southern society and government.

Wherever slavery existed, laws called slave codes helped to keep slaves under control. Among the many restrictions, slaves could not carry guns, leave their plantation or travel without written permission, or meet in groups without a white person being present. The laws also banned slave marriages and made it illegal to teach a slave to read and write.

Despite these restrictions, slave rebellions did occur. In 1739, an uprising of slaves at Stono, South Carolina, resulted in the deaths of thirty white colonists before the authorities were able to regain control. A slave revolt led by Gabriel Prosser in Virginia in 1800 and a planned revolt discovered in South Carolina in 1822 spread terror among white Southerners. In 1831, another revolt in Virginia, organized by the slave Nat Turner, lasted two months and took the lives of more than sixty white Virginians. States responded to such events by passing more and harsher slave codes.

The treatment of slaves by individual masters varied widely. Many slaveholders used beatings, reduced food rations, and threats to break up families to control and discipline their slaves. Troublemakers—or their children—might be sold to another plantation far away. Some masters, realizing that slaves were a valuable investment, treated them better. But life for most slaves was hard, especially for those who worked in the fields.

Frederick Douglass, who escaped from slavery in 1838, later described working as a field hand in Maryland:

> We were often in the field from the first approach of day til its last lingering ray had left us. . . . Covey [the master] would . . . urge us on with his words, example, and frequently the whip. . . . His work went on in his absence almost as well as in his presence. . . . He always aimed at taking us by surprise. . . . It was never safe to stop a single minute. . . . We were worked in all weathers. It was never too hot or too

Field hands worked long hours. By the early 1800s the South's economy depended on the growing of cotton, and on the labor of slaves to tend and harvest the crop.

cold; it could never rain, blow, hail, or snow, too hard for us to work in the field.[6]

Even when they were well treated, most slaves longed for freedom. A master might free a slave to reward exceptionally loyal service, or in some other unusual circumstance. But such events were rare. The slave codes generally required a freed slave to leave the state. In most cases, this meant leaving friends and family, who remained enslaved on the plantation.

Escapes were much more common. There is no way of knowing how many slaves tried to flee slavery. Estimates of successful escapes between 1800 and 1860 range from 60,000 to 100,000, with 50,000 to 75,000 occurring after 1830.[7] A number of slaves who escaped to freedom in the North became part of a growing movement there to end slavery in the United States.

3

THE ANTISLAVERY CRUSADE

From the early years of colonization until the outbreak of the Civil War in 1861, many white Americans considered slavery to be cruel and immoral. This group included some white Southerners. But most southern opponents of slavery were afraid to speak out because of the slaveholders' power and prestige.

The abolitionists, as the people who wanted to do away with, or abolish, slavery were known, were a relatively small group of white and African-American men and women. Generally Northerners, they formed organizations that often disagreed over methods and goals. Although they were not widely popular in the North, over time they caused slaveholders to unite in fear of them. For this reason, and because of their dedication to their cause, the antislavery movement had power and influence far greater than its number of supporters.

Abolition and the American Revolution

In addition to the moral argument, early opposition to slavery arose from political events. As calls for independence from Great Britain grew, the practice of slavery became an embarrassment to some patriots. They wondered how they could criticize Britain for "enslaving" the colonies when the colonists themselves held slaves. This seeming inconsistency became even greater in 1776, when the colonies declared their independence from Britain. In the Declaration of Independence, Virginia's Thomas Jefferson wrote: "We hold these truths to be self-evident, that all men are created equal, that they are endowed by their Creator with certain unalienable Rights, that among these are Life, Liberty, and the pursuit of Happiness."

However, to most Americans of the times, the equality and rights that Jefferson claimed did not apply to anyone who was not white. Most white Northerners and nearly all white Southerners believed that races other than their own were inferior. To many Americans the enslavement of inferior peoples was justified.

These prejudices created a huge challenge to colonists who linked independence and abolition. But in the North, where the economy was not built on slave labor, abolitionists were able to use the spirit of equality promised by the Revolution to begin eliminating slavery. Massachusetts, Vermont, and New Hampshire outlawed it in the constitutions that set up their state governments after independence was declared. In the 1780s, Rhode Island, Connecticut, and Pennsylvania all passed laws that required gradual emancipation, or freedom, for slaves in the state. New York enacted such a law in 1799, and New Jersey

This illustration of a slave pleading for his freedom appeared in many British and American antislavery publications in the late 1700s and early 1800s.

became the last state to voluntarily end slavery when it passed one in 1804.

Gradual-emancipation laws required that all children born to female slaves after a certain date be freed when they reached twenty-one to twenty-five years of age. But the mothers of these children, and all other slaves born before the laws' date, remained enslaved for life. Thus slavery did not completely die out in the North until the 1830s and 1840s.

In the South, the abolitionists' arguments and the spirit of independence convinced some slaveholders to voluntarily free their slaves. But in the 1790s, slaves and former slaves on the nearby Caribbean island of Hispaniola successfully rebelled against French rule. This event, coupled with the plan for a slave revolt that was uncovered in Virginia in 1800, soon ended most Southerners' cooperation with voluntary emancipation. New laws made it illegal in most of the South.

Slavery and the Constitution

During the American Revolution, the Continental Congress wrote a constitution for the nation that Americans were fighting to create. Called the Articles of Confederation, this first constitution put Congress in charge of the U.S. government and gave each state one vote in running the nation's affairs. Since slaveholders were powerful in only six of the thirteen states, Congress was controlled by states where slavery was not strong.

As soon as the Revolution ended, abolitionists began to pressure the national government to take action against slavery. In 1787, Congress passed the Northwest Ordinance, which outlawed slavery in the region west of the Appalachian Mountains and north of the Ohio River. Five new states—Ohio (1803), Indiana (1816), Illinois (1818), Michigan (1837), and Wisconsin (1848)—would eventually be created from this territory.

While Congress was crafting the Northwest Ordinance, representatives of the states were meeting nearby and writing a new constitution to replace the Articles of Confederation. The fifty-five delegates to the Constitutional Convention included abolitionists as well as slaveholders. Although slavery was never directly mentioned in the Constitution of the United States, it became a major issue at the convention.

After much debate, the convention delegates decided to change the structure of Congress. They created two legislative bodies. In one, the Senate, each state would have two votes. The controversy arose over the other body, the House of Representatives, where each state's number of votes would depend on its population.

The Constitution also gave Congress increased power. Southerners feared that the northern states would use this power to attack slavery. The North already would have a seven-to-six advantage in the Senate. And the Northwest Ordinance guaranteed that at least five more "free states"—states that prohibited slavery—would someday be part of the Union. So

African captives faced harsh and crowded conditions aboard ship on the long voyage to a life of slavery in North America.

Southerners were determined to control the House of Representatives. They wanted slaves to be counted with a state's white population in determining how many representatives it would have in the House. Northern delegates insisted that slaves should not be included in a state's population. Finally, a compromise was reached. Each slave would be counted as three-fifths of a person in determining a state's representation.

However, some Southerners still feared that the national government would take some action against slavery. They demanded guarantees that they could continue to import slaves from Africa and the Caribbean. Northern delegates were willing to include a provision in the Constitution that protected the slave trade for at least twenty more years:

> The Migration or Importation of such Persons as any of the States now existing think proper to admit, shall not be prohibited by Congress prior to the Year one thousand eight hundred and eight, but a Tax or duty may be imposed on such Importation, not exceeding ten dollars for each Person.[1]

In another part of the Constitution, the delegates added the following language to further protect the institution of slavery:

> No Person held to Service or Labour in one State, under the Laws thereof, escaping into another, shall, in Consequence of any Law or Regulation therein, be discharged from such Service or Labour, but shall be delivered up on Claim of the Party to whom such Service or Labor may be due.[2]

Because many people at the time believed that slavery was dying, the abolitionists accepted these protections for it in the Constitution. However, after the cotton gin revived the South's economy, some abolitionists came to view these protections as a victory for slaveholders and slavery.

The Decline and Rebirth of Emancipation

By the early 1800s, the antislavery movement was in trouble. Congress had passed a law ending the importing of slaves in 1808. But because of cotton,

Despite his mild appearance, William Lloyd Garrison was among the most committed and radical abolitionists. This portrait was made in 1833, the year he helped to found the American Anti-Slavery Society.

slavery was expanding. Slaveholders were no longer willing to listen to appeals that they end an institution that was profitable again. Nor were they willing to free into their midst African Americans who might spark revolts among those who remained enslaved. To make matters worse, emancipated slaves were also unwelcome in many places in the North. Most Northerners feared that their presence would reduce job opportunities for whites.

In 1817, a group of antislavery crusaders attempted to address both problems by founding the American Colonization Society (ACS). The organization's goal was to purchase the freedom of slaves and to colonize them, and other free African Americans, on land the society owned in Africa. The ACS had little success, however. Most free African Americans, and some white abolitionists, considered forcing freed slaves to leave the United States to be wrong. In addition, the organization never was able to raise the funds it needed. In 1827, it asked Congress for money. But a group of southern congressmen blocked the request, arguing that the South needed its slaves.

Some moderate Northerners—Abraham Lincoln among them—continued to support colonization until the Civil War. But by the 1830s, more radical calls for emancipation were being heard. A new generation of young abolitionists considered colonization too slow and ineffective. They demanded quick and drastic action to bring slavery to an end.

In part, these calls resulted from events elsewhere in the world. Inspired by the American Revolution, Spain's Latin American colonies declared their independence in the early 1800s. After gaining their freedom, they all either abolished slavery outright or enacted gradual emancipation laws. Then, in 1833, Great Britain abolished slavery throughout its empire. This ended slavery in its Caribbean colonies as well as in Canada. American abolitionists were embarrassed that the United States and Brazil were the only two nations in the Western Hemisphere where slavery continued to thrive.

The Growth of Abolitionism

On January 1, 1831, a new weekly newspaper appeared in Boston, Massachusetts. Named the *Liberator,* it was dedicated to the cause of abolition. Its publisher, twenty-five-year-old William Lloyd Garrison, already was known as a radical foe of slavery. He had recently returned from Maryland, where he had served nearly two months in jail for writing an antislavery article in a Baltimore newspaper. The editorial that Garrison wrote for the first issue of the *Liberator* showed that imprisonment had not changed his tactics or his views:

> I am aware that many object to the severity of my language; but is there not cause for severity? I will be as harsh as truth, and as uncompromising as justice. On this subject, I do not wish to think, or speak, or write, with moderation. No! no! Tell a man whose house is on fire, to give a moderate alarm; . . . tell the mother to gradually extricate [remove] her babe from the fire into which it has fallen;—but urge me not to use moderation in a cause like the present. I am in earnest—I will not equivocate [sidestep]—I will not excuse—I will not retreat a single inch—AND I WILL BE HEARD.[3]

In 1833, Garrison, New York, businessmen Arthur and Lewis Tappan, and some sixty other white and African-American men and women, gathered in Philadelphia, Pennsylvania, to found the American Anti-Slavery Society. Within two years hundreds of state and local branches of the society formed in the North. These groups flooded the North and South

Frederick Douglass was but one of many African Americans who worked to end slavery in the United States.

with antislavery literature. They collected hundreds of thousands of signatures on petitions to Congress demanding action against slavery. They paid lecturers to crisscross the North, speaking about the evils of slavery. They also cooperated with the Underground Railroad, a secret network of abolitionists who helped slaves escape to the North and Canada.

Some of the most effective abolitionists were themselves escaped slaves. After Harriet Tubman fled slavery, she sneaked back into the South at least fifteen times to lead others to freedom. Twenty-four-year-old Frederick Douglass had been free for just three years when he became a lecturer for the American

SOURCE DOCUMENT

FELLOW-CITIZENS, PARDON ME, ALLOW ME TO ASK, WHY AM I CALLED UPON TO SPEAK HERE TO-DAY? WHAT HAVE I, OR THOSE I REPRESENT, TO DO WITH YOUR NATIONAL INDEPENDENCE? ARE THE GREAT PRINCIPLES OF POLITICAL FREEDOM AND NATURAL JUSTICE, EMBODIED IN THAT DECLARATION OF INDEPENDENCE, EXTENDED TO US? . . . THIS FOURTH OF JULY IS *YOURS*, NOT *MINE*. *YOU* MAY REJOICE, *I* MUST MOURN. . . .

FELLOW-CITIZENS, ABOVE YOUR NATIONAL, TUMULTUOUS JOY, I HEAR THE MOURNFUL WAIL OF MILLIONS! WHOSE CHAINS, HEAVY AND GRIEVOUS YESTERDAY, ARE, TO-DAY, RENDERED MORE INTOLERABLE BY THE JUBILEE SHOUTS THAT REACH THEM. . . .

WHAT, TO THE AMERICAN SLAVE, IS YOUR 4TH OF JULY? I ANSWER; A DAY THAT REVEALS TO HIM, MORE THAN ALL OTHER DAYS OF THE YEAR, THE GROSS INJUSTICE AND CRUELTY TO WHICH HE IS THE CONSTANT VICTIM. TO HIM, YOUR CELEBRATION IS A SHAM; . . . YOUR SOUNDS OF REJOICING ARE EMPTY AND HEARTLESS; . . . YOUR SHOUTS OF LIBERTY AND EQUALITY, HOLLOW MOCKERY. . . .

In 1852, black abolitionist Frederick Douglass was asked to give a speech at the Fourth of July celebration in Rochester, New York. Douglass used the occasion to remind his listeners that not all Americans had cause to celebrate the holiday.

Anti-Slavery Society. His striking appearance, powerful voice, and eloquent descriptions of slavery soon made him famous and a leader of the movement.

But despite their devotion and hard work, the abolitionists did not accomplish their goals. A gag rule pushed through the House of Representatives by Southerners kept the House from discussing the thousands of petitions the abolitionists sent to Congress. The pamphlets and newspapers they mailed to Southerners also were not effective. Before long, every southern state had passed a law forbidding the delivery of antislavery literature. The few brave individuals who visited the South to present the message in person were beaten or jailed.

Even in the North, people opposed to abolitionism frequently pelted antislavery speakers with rocks or raw eggs. Mobs broke up abolitionist meetings and damaged the churches and other buildings where they were held. The Tappan brothers were attacked on the street in New York. Their homes and place of business were nearly destroyed. In Boston, Garrison's activities attracted so much anger that in 1835, he was seized by a mob. Only quick action by city officials kept him from being killed. In Alton, Illinois, a mob killed Elijah Lovejoy in 1837, when he refused to stop publishing his antislavery newspaper.

Although the abolitionists remained unpopular, their suffering did help convert more Northerners to their cause. It also convinced some abolitionists to become even more extreme. In the 1840s, Garrison joined Wendell Phillips, another well-known white abolitionist, and prominent black abolitionist Charles Remond in attacking the Constitution for protecting slavery. Henry Garnet, another former slave, began urging slaves to revolt:

Brethren, arise, arise! Strike for your lives and liberties. Now is the day and the hour. . . . Remember that you are FOUR MILLIONS! It is in your power so to torment the God-cursed slaveholders that they will be glad to let you go free.[4]

White Southerners claimed that such words and ideas proved abolitionists were dangerous radicals. The South became even more determined to resist attempts to end slavery.

Garrison and his friends even frightened other abolitionists. His extremism, along with his calls for equal rights for women and African Americans, led to a second split in the antislavery movement in the 1840s. Within a few years, however, other events had shifted most Americans' attention from the abolition of slavery to issues surrounding its spread into new territories.

Slavery in the Territories

Between 1800 and 1850, the size of the United States more than doubled. In 1803, President Thomas Jefferson purchased the Louisiana Territory from France. This huge region extended from the present-day state of Louisiana north up the Mississippi River to Canada, and west to the Rocky Mountains. As cotton production increased and the plantation system spread after Whitney's invention of the cotton gin, questions arose about whether slavery would be permitted on these vast new lands.

In 1820, Northerners and Southerners in Congress struck a deal on this issue. Missouri, the second state

Abolitionist gatherings were sometimes attacked by angry mobs, as was this antislavery meeting in Boston.

formed from the territory (Louisiana was the first) would enter the Union as a slave state. But only the region south of Missouri would be open to slavery in the future. In all other parts of the Louisiana Territory, slavery was to be banned forever. This agreement, which also admitted Maine as a free state, became known as the Missouri Compromise. It settled the status of slavery on all land that was part of the United States at the time. But Jefferson, an ex-president by 1820, warned that the Missouri Compromise would not be a permanent solution to the slavery issue. His prediction proved to be right.

Arkansas joined Louisiana and Missouri in 1836 as the only slave states formed from the Louisiana

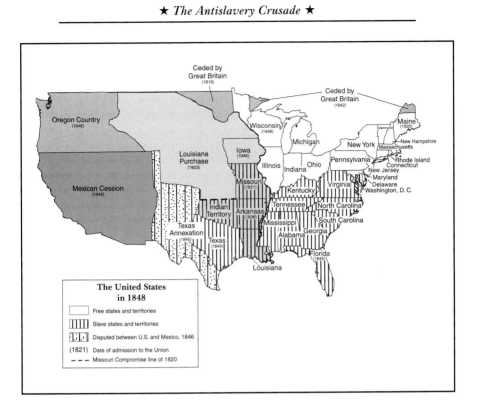

The expansion of the United States required the question of slavery in new lands to be addressed. Until the Mexican War brought more territory in 1848, the Missouri Compromise of 1820 settled this issue. But it arose again when the Mexican Cession was added.

Territory. Meanwhile, some Southerners had pushed farther west with their slaves. They settled in Texas, which was then part of Mexico. In 1836, Texas won its freedom from Mexico and became an independent nation. Almost at once, slaveholders in the United States and Texas began seeking its admission to the Union. After years of northern opposition, southern congressmen finally succeeded in gaining statehood for Texas in 1845.

When Texas entered the Union, its border with Mexico was still in dispute. In 1846, President James Polk, a slaveholder from Tennessee, sent American troops into the disputed territory and provoked a war with Mexico. Two years later, the defeated Mexicans turned over California and most of what is now the American Southwest to the United States.

Many opponents of slavery saw the war with Mexico as a southern scheme to gain more land for the plantation system. This suspicion caused Pennsylvania congressman David Wilmot to offer an amendment to a bill that provided money needed to fight the war. His amendment proposed banning slavery in any territory the United States gained from Mexico as a result of the war.

Although the House of Representatives passed Wilmot's amendment, it was defeated in the Senate, where the southern states and the northern states had an equal number of votes. But the Wilmot Proviso, as the proposal was known, aroused great concern in the South. It was the first time that either house of Congress had passed a measure against slavery.

Following congressional elections in 1846, Wilmot introduced his proposal into the new Congress in 1847. Although it again failed in the Senate, it passed the House a second time. Among its supporters on this occasion was a newly-elected congressman from Illinois. His name was Abraham Lincoln.

Abraham Lincoln hated slavery all his adult life. Yet he never became an abolitionist. This fact illustrates how complicated the slavery issue was for him, especially in his professional and political careers. On one hand, he felt strongly that slavery was wrong. However, he also knew that it was lawful and was protected by the Constitution—which, as both an attorney and an elected official, he was sworn to uphold.

THE LONE STAR OF ILLINOIS

As Lincoln became more involved in politics, the problem of slavery grew even more difficult for him. He had to find a position on the issue that did not violate his deeply held personal beliefs, but which also would not turn the majority of voters against him.

Boyhood Experiences with Slavery

Abraham Lincoln was born in a log cabin about fifty miles south of Louisville, in what is now LaRue County, Kentucky, on February 12, 1809. At the time of his birth, about 1,600 whites and 1,000 enslaved African Americans lived in the area.[1] But Lincoln's parents were poor, and, like most white Southerners, they held no slaves.

It is not clear when Lincoln's feelings about slavery first developed. When he was two years old, his father bought a farm on the main road between Louisville and Nashville, Tennessee. So it is likely that the impressionable little boy saw caravans of people in chains passing by the door of the family's home.[2] His views were also probably influenced by his parents. The minister of the church they attended was openly opposed to slavery. As a youth, Abe no doubt heard about slavery's sinfulness both in church and at home. These early influences may account for his statement, years later as president, that "I am naturally anti-slavery. . . . I can not remember when I did not so think, and feel."[3]

Partly because of their opposition to slavery, the Lincolns left Kentucky in 1816, when Abe was seven years old. The family moved to Indiana Territory, arriving just weeks before the territory became the nineteenth state of the Union. They settled in what is now Spencer County, not far from the Ohio River and about seventy-five miles west of Louisville. Young Abe helped his father build a cabin and clear enough land for a small wilderness farm.

Even though slavery had been banned in Indiana by the Northwest Ordinance of 1787, not all the state's people were opposed to it. Debates over slavery swirled around the growing boy. The frequent presence of slave-catchers in his southern Indiana region, hunting down runaway slaves who had escaped across the Ohio River to freedom, also may have affected Lincoln's developing views about the peculiar institution.

In 1828, the nineteen-year-old Lincoln took a job on a boat carrying farm produce down the Ohio and Mississippi rivers from Indiana to New Orleans, Louisiana. During a month's stay in that city, he was exposed to the everyday practice of slavery. He read the

Young Abe Lincoln probably witnessed African Americans being moved in handcuffs and leg irons, such as this slave caravan in 1815.

advertisements of slave dealers in the newspaper and even attended a slave auction. There Lincoln witnessed men and women being bought and sold like livestock. He saw the pens where they were held while awaiting their turn on the auction block. More than twenty years later, the shock of these revelations still affected him. "I saw it all [for] myself," Lincoln recalled in 1851, "and the horrid pictures are in my mind yet."[4]

Slavery in Lincoln's Early Political Career

In 1830, the family moved again, settling in Macon County, Illinois, just north of what is now the city of Decatur. The next year, the twenty-two-year-old Lincoln set out on his own. After a second boat trip to New Orleans, he took a job as a store clerk in New Salem, a village about twenty miles northwest of Springfield, Illinois. His kindness and honesty quickly made him a well-known figure in the community.

Lincoln's popularity encouraged him in 1832 to run for the Illinois legislature as a representative from Sangamon County. He ran as a Whig—a political party that was one of the forerunners to today's Republican party. "Fellow citizens, I presume you all know who I am. I am humble Abraham Lincoln," he declared as he campaigned across the county. "If elected, I shall be thankful."[5]

Although most of Lincoln's New Salem neighbors voted for him, he lost the county-wide election. In 1834, he ran again, and this time he won! In December, the twenty-five-year-old took his seat for the first of what would be four terms in the Illinois General Assembly.

One of the other newly-elected legislators in 1834 was a Springfield attorney named John Stuart. Stuart encouraged Lincoln to become an attorney and loaned him books so he could study the law.

In those times a person did not have to go to college in order to become an attorney. Many people who wanted to be lawyers, particularly if they lived in rural or frontier regions, learned the law by studying books on their own and from attorneys who were already in practice. Lincoln took this approach and read law books whenever the legislature was not in session. In 1836, after two years of intense study, he passed the test required of would-be attorneys and was issued a license to practice law in Illinois. The following year, he joined Stuart's law office in Springfield, which had just become the new capital of Illinois.

While Lincoln established his law practice, he was also establishing his position on the issue of slavery. In 1837, the Illinois legislature overwhelmingly passed a resolution attacking the abolition movement. Lincoln joined one other legislator in protesting the resolution. "The institution of slavery is founded on both injustice and bad policy," they wrote. But they also observed that "the Congress of the United States has no power, under the constitution, to interfere with the institution of slavery in the different States."[6] In addition, they were careful in their protest to attack the abolitionists for increasing the tensions surrounding the slavery issue.

At auctions such as this one, slaves were sold to the highest bidder with little regard for family ties. Wives and husbands were separated, as were children and parents. A slave might be bought by someone who lived hundreds of miles from the rest of the slave's family.

This protest document shows that Lincoln was already becoming a clever politician. The protest publicly established his dislike of slavery. At the same time, however, the document made it clear that Lincoln was not an abolitionist. He was trying to establish a "middle" position on the issue that he hoped would satisfy proslavery and antislavery voters alike.

Lincoln took a similar stance after the murder of abolitionist newspaper editor Elijah Lovejoy in Alton, Illinois, in November 1837. In his reaction, he was careful to condemn the mob's action without directly supporting the cause for which Lovejoy gave his life:

Whenever the vicious portion of population shall be permitted to gather in bands [and] . . . throw printing presses into rivers, shoot editors, and hang and burn obnoxious persons at pleasure . . . this Government cannot last. . . . There is no grievance that is a fit object of redress [correction] by mob law. In any case that arises, as for instance, the promulgation [issue] of abolitionism, one of two positions is necessarily true; that is, the thing is right . . . and therefore deserves the protection of all law . . . ; or, it is wrong, and therefore proper to be prohibited by legal enactments; and in neither case, is the interposition [use] of mob law, either necessary, justifiable, or excusable.[7]

In 1839, Lincoln helped defeat a resolution in the Illinois legislature that supported the continuation of slavery in Washington, D.C. But he sought to straddle both sides of this issue, too, arguing that slavery should be abolished in the nation's capital only if the majority of the city's citizens asked for such a ban.[8]

Slavery and the Practice of Law

After eight years as a state legislator, Lincoln returned to private life in 1841. In part, this was due to events that developed in his courtship of twenty-one-year-old Mary Todd, John Stuart's cousin and the daughter of a wealthy Kentucky slaveholder. After accepting Lincoln's marriage proposal in 1840, Todd openly and repeatedly flirted with Stephen A. Douglas, another Springfield attorney. Upset and insecure, Lincoln broke their engagement.[9]

After more than a year apart, the couple finally did reconcile, and they were married in November 1842.

But Lincoln's deep depression over his failed romance interfered with his ability to carry out his legislative duties throughout 1841. When his term expired, he decided not to seek re-election and to instead focus on the practice of law.

As an attorney, Lincoln tried to avoid cases that dealt with slavery. But he did allow himself to become involved in two such disputes. His choice of these cases once again suggests his desire not to be publicly linked with only one side of the slavery issue. In 1841, Lincoln represented a young black woman who had been sold into slavery while living in Illinois. He won the case by arguing that because slavery was illegal in the state, no person could be bought or sold there.

Six years later, Lincoln took the opposite position by representing a slaveholder who brought his slaves from Kentucky to work on a farm he owned in southern Illinois. With the help of local abolitionists, the slaves escaped and sued for their freedom. Lincoln argued that because the slaves were in Illinois only temporarily, the state's ban on slavery did not apply. The court rejected this reasoning and ruled against Lincoln's client, who returned to Kentucky without his slaves and without paying his lawyer![10]

Lincoln Goes to Congress

At first, Lincoln's political career seemed over when he left the legislature. Running for another state office was not practical. Although the region around Springfield supported the Whigs, the Democratic party dominated the rest of the state. The governor and all other statewide officeholders were Democrats. Running for Congress was also out of the question because the region's seat in the House of Representatives was held by Lincoln's former law partner and fellow Whig John Stuart.

After the census of 1840, however, the U.S. House of Representatives created another congressional district in central Illinois because of the population growth that had occurred there. Party leaders decided that Lincoln and two other important local Whigs should share this new House seat by each occupying it for one term.

In 1846, it was Lincoln's turn to run. His election made him the only Illinois Whig in Congress. When he took his seat in 1847, the war between the United States and Mexico was drawing to a close. He gained the attention of congressional leaders by making speeches attacking President Polk, a slaveholding Democrat, for starting the war. But the new congressman had nothing to say about the issue the war created—whether to allow slavery in new territory gained from Mexico.

During his one term in the House, Lincoln voted for the Wilmot Proviso, which unsuccessfully sought to ban slavery on land acquired from Mexico, each time it came up for consideration. However, he did not participate in any of the angry debates over the issues that were taking place in Congress. Lincoln's noticeable silence in this dispute, about which he

Lincoln was in his thirties when he posed for this photo in the mid-1840s. Although the exact year is unknown, this is among the earliest photographs made.

obviously had strong feelings, resulted from his concerns about the future of his party.

By the late 1840s, southern Whigs were demanding that their party defend slavery. They hoped this would convince southern voters to elect Whigs instead of Democrats. But other Whigs were pushing the party to take a stand against slavery. They were worried about holding on to northeastern Whigs, who were deserting to join the Free-Soil party, a new political party that opposed the spread of slavery.

The Whigs' struggle over slavery allowed Lincoln, a one-term congressman from a state where his party had little influence, to quickly rise to a position of party leadership. This development, in turn, helped him to become known outside the state of Illinois.

Saving the Whigs

In 1848, Abraham Lincoln was among a small group of politicians who controlled the fate of one of the nation's two major parties. His position on the slavery issue that was threatening to destroy the Whigs was a moderate one. He had first expressed it as a state legislator in the 1830s and, with some minor changes, it remained his guiding principle on the subject for the rest of his life.

According to Lincoln, Congress had the right to regulate slavery in the territories and in the nation's capital, but only the states had control over slavery within their borders. He favored the end of slavery where it existed, but he believed that Congress did not have the constitutional authority to accomplish this. However, his unwavering support of the Wilmot Proviso showed that he wanted Congress to prevent slavery's spread into the territories.

Lincoln saw his position as a way to save the Whig party. He hoped that southern Whigs who wanted slavery defended, and northern Whigs who opposed slavery, could each get enough satisfaction from his views to hold the party together. In 1848, the Whigs needed a presidential candidate who accepted these views and who would be popular with the voters. In finding such a candidate, Lincoln pushed his party in an unusual direction.

It may seem strange that a man who opposed the war with Mexico would support the leading figure in that war as his party's candidate for president in 1848. But to Lincoln, General Zachary Taylor seemed ideal. As the commander who had led American troops to victory in several major battles, Taylor was a war hero. As a slaveholder, he would appeal to southern voters. But he also opposed the spread of slavery. This would appeal to many voters in the North.

Lincoln, along with southern Whigs Alexander Stephens of Georgia and John Crittenden of Kentucky, helped to gain Taylor's nomination as the Whig's presidential candidate in 1848. He also played a major role in Taylor's campaign. In November, Taylor was elected president. But Lincoln's joy was soon replaced by disillusionment and despair. True to the agreement he had made with Whig leaders in

Illinois, he did not seek a second term in Congress. However, Taylor did not reward him with the job he wanted—heading the government's Land Office. A few weeks after his fortieth birthday, a disappointed Lincoln returned to private life in Springfield, Illinois.

Another blow occurred in 1850, as Congress tried to finally settle the issue of slavery in the territory gained in the war. At the height of the crisis, President Taylor, who opposed the spread of slavery, ate some spoiled food at a Fourth of July picnic and died. Within two years the Whig party began to dissolve. Lincoln, the man whose loyalty caused some Whigs to call him the "Lone Star of Illinois," found himself with no party and no political future.

Colonization and Compensated Emancipation

From 1849 to 1854, Lincoln concentrated on the practice of law. But he still found time to reflect on slavery. Following Taylor's death, Northerners and Southerners in Congress had finally agreed on slavery in the land acquired from Mexico as part of a larger settlement called the Compromise of 1850. The agreement was that the people of the region would decide whether to allow slavery through "popular sovereignty"—a process by which the people of each area would themselves decide whether to allow slavery.

At the time, the Compromise of 1850 seemed to bring the controversy over slavery's expansion to an end. So Lincoln began to think about how slavery might be attacked legally in places where it already existed. Curiously, he settled on two old and widely discredited solutions: pay slaveholders money to give up their slaves—called "compensated emancipation"— and colonize the freed slaves in Africa.

Compensated emancipation overcame one of the constitutional protections of slavery—the property-rights clause of the Fifth Amendment, which guarantees that "private property [shall not] be taken . . . without just compensation." Lincoln reasoned that colonizing the freed African Americans out of the country would make both northern and southern whites more accepting of his plan. It would remove free blacks, a group that white Southerners considered the most troublesome element in their society, without sending them north to compete with white workers for jobs.

Of course, Lincoln's plan was totally impractical. Southern slaveholders were no more willing to give up their slaves than enslaved African Americans—nearly all of whom had been born and raised in the United States—were willing to be relocated to Africa.

Lincoln's Return to Politics

When Lincoln became a congressman in 1847, his old romantic rival Stephen Douglas became U.S. senator from Illinois. But while Lincoln returned home in 1849, Senator Douglas, a Democrat, became a national figure by helping to shape the Compromise of 1850. Soon, Douglas began to think about running for president. To

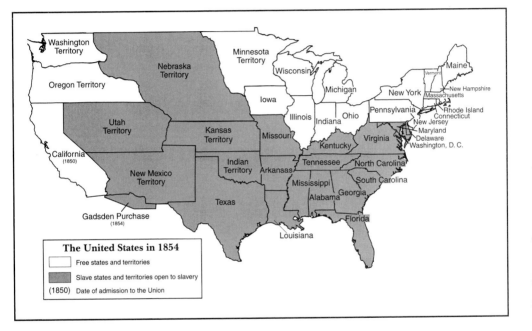

The United States in 1854

Free states and territories

Slave states and territories open to slavery

(1850) Date of admission to the Union

In the Compromise of 1850, Congress allowed people living in the former Mexican territories to decide the slavery issue themselves. But the Kansas-Nebraska Act, which allowed the same process north of the Missouri Compromise line, outraged abolitionists.

further his ambitions, he pushed a law through Congress in 1854 that pulled Abraham Lincoln back into politics.

The Kansas-Nebraska Act opened the territory west of Missouri for settlement and eventual admission as states in the Union. In writing the act, Douglas included two controversial provisions. One required the question of slavery in Kansas to be settled by the people who lived there—in other words, by popular sovereignty. And because Kansas was part of the region forever closed to slavery by the Missouri Compromise of 1820, the bill's other controversial provision repealed the Missouri Compromise!

Douglas thought that putting popular sovereignty into his bill would gain it enough support from northern and southern senators to allow it to pass. In this strategy he was right. But by repealing the Missouri Compromise, the Kansas-Nebraska Act again exposed the entire Louisiana Purchase to slavery. It also reopened the bitter controversy over the spread of slavery

Douglas's law created a firestorm of protest across the North. Major changes in American politics occurred as public debate over the law split the Democratic and Whig parties. Antislavery Democrats left their party and joined with northern Whigs and Free-Soilers to found the Republican party.

Lincoln described himself as "thunderstruck and stunned" by the Kansas-Nebraska Act.[11] The renewed controversy over slavery awakened his desire to return to public office. But he soon realized that he could not

SOURCE DOCUMENT

To illustrate the case—Abraham Lincoln has a fine meadow . . . well fenced, which John Calhoun had agreed with Abraham (originally owning the land in common) should be his. . . . John Calhoun, however, in the course of time, had become owner of an extensive herd of cattle. . . . Calhoun then looks with a longing eye on Lincoln's meadow, and goes to it and throws down the fences. . . . "You rascal," says Lincoln, "what have you done? What did you do this for?"—"Oh," replies Calhoun, "everything is right. I have taken down your fence; but nothing more. It is my true intent and meaning not to drive my cattle into your meadow . . . but to leave them perfectly free . . . To direct their movements in their own way."

Now would not the man who committed this outrage be . . . a fool in supposing that there could be one man found in the country to believe that he had not pulled down the fence for the purpose of opening the meadow for his cattle?

In September 1854, Lincoln wrote to the Illinois Journal *in Springfield. He argued that the Kansas-Nebraska Act betrayed earlier agreements on the spread of slavery. To help readers understand his points, he compared Kansas to a meadow and the act to the destruction of the meadow's fence, which represents the Missouri Compromise.*

accomplish this goal through the Whig party, which was now nearly dead. So when Illinois opponents of slavery founded a state Republican party in 1856, Lincoln was among its organizers.

Once again, Lincoln rapidly rose to a leadership position in his party. In 1858, Illinois Republicans chose him as their candidate to oppose Douglas, who was seeking a third term in the Senate. Lincoln's acceptance of their nomination produced what was probably the most important speech of his political career. It focused on what would be the main issue of his campaign—the slavery controversy in Kansas and Nebraska. Quoting the Bible, Lincoln made a dire prediction.

"A house divided against itself cannot stand." I believe this government cannot endure, permanently half *slave* and half *free*. I do not expect the Union to be *dissolved*—I do not expect the house to *fall*—but I *do* expect it will cease to be divided. It will become *all* one thing, or *all* the other.[12]

Illinois senator Stephen Douglas was known as the "Little Giant" because of his great political power and small size. At well under 6 feet, he appeared even shorter when standing next to the nearly 6'6" Lincoln.

This statement was viewed as the most radical threat against slavery yet made by any Republican leader. It suggested that Lincoln's real plans for slavery went far beyond opposition to its spread. So the speech attracted great attention. For months afterward, Lincoln tried to explain what he had meant. "I did not say I was in favor of anything," he told a journalist. "I made a prediction only—it may have been a foolish one perhaps."[13] But from then on, Lincoln was unable to convince Southerners that he was not an abolitionist.

Despite all the trouble the "house-divided" speech caused him, it made Abraham Lincoln a national figure. When he and Douglas faced off in debates in seven Illinois towns during the 1858 campaign, thousands of people gathered at each place to hear them speak. The Lincoln-Douglas debates were widely reported in newspapers outside the state. People across the nation became aware of each candidate's views on slavery.

Stephen Douglas was returned to the Senate in 1858. But Lincoln was the real winner of their contest. Statements that Douglas made during the debates caused him to lose support in both North and South. At the same time, Lincoln's moderate positions increased his standing among Northerners. Thus Douglas's prospects of becoming president decreased. Lincoln, however, emerged from the debates as one of the nation's best-known Republicans and a contender for his party's presidential nomination in 1860.

5

NOW IS THE TIME

In 1860, Illinois citizen Abraham Lincoln became the Republican candidate for president of the United States. The Democratic party nominated Illinois senator Stephen Douglas. But Southerners were still upset over Douglas's statements during the Lincoln-Douglas debates of 1858. This, combined with the party's refusal to openly support slavery, caused some southern Democrats to reject Douglas. They selected John Breckinridge, a slaveholder from Kentucky, as their presidential candidate. Others turned to Tennessee's John Bell of the newly formed Constitutional Union party.

This split among the Democrats allowed Lincoln to be elected in November 1860 with not even 40 percent of the vote. Most worrisome was that of the 1,865,000 votes he received, only 26,000 came from voters in states that allowed slavery.[1]

A Critical Waiting Period

In the 1800s, a newly elected president did not take office until March—four months after the November election. (Today, presidents are inaugurated in

January.) Lincoln remained at home in Springfield, preparing to take office.

Newspaper editors wrote to the president-elect, asking for a statement that would calm the nation's fears during this waiting period. But Lincoln believed that providing such a statement would only make matters worse. "I could say nothing which I have not already said," he replied to one request. Repeating his position on slavery would make him appear weak, he said, which would cost him the respect of "good men, and encourage bad ones to clamor the more loudly."[2]

Even as South Carolina formally withdrew from the United States in December 1860, Lincoln maintained his public silence. Privately, however, he tried to convince southern leaders that slaveholders had nothing to fear. "Do the people of the South really entertain fears that a Republican administration would, *directly,* or *indirectly*, interfere with their slaves . . . ?" he asked Georgia's Alexander Stephens (who later became vice president of the Confederacy). "If they do, I wish to assure you . . . that there is no cause for such fears."[3]

At the same time Lincoln was promising that he would take no action against slavery where it existed, he also made it clear that he would not permit its spread. Hoping to prevent the breakup of the nation, a number of leaders proposed compromises that would allow slavery in some of the nation's territories. When he learned of these efforts, Lincoln wrote to a Republican member of Congress:

Prevent, as far as possible, any of our friends from . . . entertaining propositions for compromise of any sort, on *"slavery extension."* There is no possible compromise upon it. . . . On that point hold firm, as with a chain of steel.[4]

Lincoln considered differences over slavery in the territories to be a poor reason for hostility between North and South. But many Southerners disagreed. As efforts at compromise collapsed, six more southern states—Mississippi, Louisiana, Alabama, Georgia, Florida, and Texas—left the Union. By the time Lincoln arrived in Washington, D.C., these states had joined South Carolina to form the Confederate States of America, also called the Confederacy.

On March 4, 1861, Abraham Lincoln became president of the United States. He repeated his pledge to protect slavery in his Inaugural Address: "I have no purpose, directly or indirectly, to interfere with the institution of slavery in the States where it exists. I believe I have no lawful right to do so, and I have no inclination [desire] to do so."[5]

However, he warned Southerners that "no State, upon its own mere motion, can lawfully get out of the Union," and that "*you* have no oath registered in Heaven to destroy the government, while *I* shall have the most solemn one to 'preserve, protect, and defend' it."[6] These two principles—that the president had no right to interfere with slavery where it existed and that the president had every right to preserve the nation—set the tone for the first eighteen months of the Civil War.

The inauguration of Abraham Lincoln took place on the steps of the Capitol in 1861, just as it does for incoming presidents today.

The Civil War Begins

As the southern states seceded, they took over post offices, forts, and other U.S. government property within their borders. One of the few places that held out was Fort Sumter, on an island in the harbor of Charleston, South Carolina. Southerners decided that they would starve the fort's troops into surrendering. In April 1861, however, Lincoln announced that the navy would resupply Fort Sumter by sea. Confederate forces attacked and captured the fort before the supplies could arrive.

Lincoln responded to the attack on Fort Sumter by proclaiming that a rebellion existed in the seven seceded states. He called up 75,000 state militiamen (citizen-soldiers similar to today's National Guard) to put down the uprising. Four more slave states—Virginia, North Carolina, Tennessee, and Arkansas—then joined the Confederacy rather than provide troops to fight fellow Southerners.

In the North, many abolitionists were pleased by these events. They believed the South's actions gave the government a reason to take forceful and drastic action to end slavery. "Thank God!" cried abolitionist Frederick Douglass.

> The slaveholders themselves have saved our cause from ruin! They have exposed the throat of slavery to the keen knife of liberty, and have given a chance to all the righteous forces of the nation to deal a death-blow to the monster evil of the nineteenth century.—*Friends of freedom! be up and doing;—now is your time.* The tyrant's extremity [moment of destruction] is your opportunity! . . . Now is the day, and now is the hour![7]

The abolitionists' joy was short-lived, however. In July 1861, a Union army left Washington, D.C., and marched into Virginia. Its goal was to capture the Confederate capital at Richmond and end the war. The Northerners had traveled only about twenty miles when they were met and beaten by a smaller southern force near a creek called Bull Run. Congress immediately passed a resolution stating that the goal of the war was not to overthrow slavery, but to preserve the Union. Lincoln reasoned that after this battlefield defeat, support for the war would be better sustained by the spirit of patriotism than by any opposition to slavery.

Slavery, Emancipation, and the Border States

Another reason that Lincoln resisted the abolitionists' calls was his concern over the border states. Four slave states—Missouri, Kentucky, Maryland, and Delaware—had not seceded from the Union. Slavery was not important in Delaware, where fewer than 2,000 of the state's 112,000 people were enslaved. But Missouri, Kentucky, and Maryland were home to more than 425,000 slaves.

Because these three states now bordered the Confederacy, their loyalty was vital to the nation. Control of Missouri and Kentucky was important to travel on the upper Mississippi and Ohio Rivers. Maryland was especially critical. The District of Columbia was located between Maryland and Virginia. If Maryland seceded, Washington would be cut off from the United States and surrounded by Confederate territory.

Most citizens in the border states supported the Union cause. But their support was for the restoration of the nation, not for the abolition of slavery. Lincoln did not want to take any action that might encourage any of these states to leave the Union.

For example, in Missouri some slaveholders who sympathized with the South were stirring up unrest

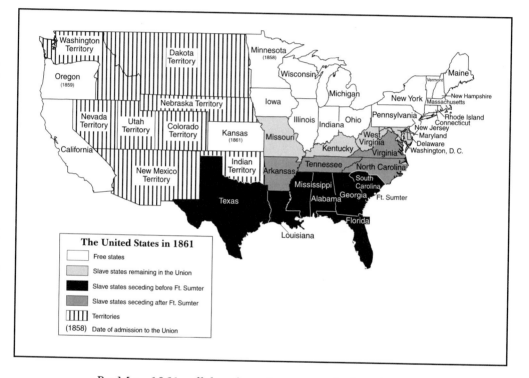

The United States in 1861

- Free states
- Slave states remaining in the Union
- Slave states seceding before Ft. Sumter
- Slave states seceding after Ft. Sumter
- Territories
- (1858) Date of admission to the Union

By May 1861, all but four slave states had withdrawn from the Union. However, people in the western counties of Virginia did not agree with their state's action and in 1863 they were admitted to the Union as the state of West Virginia.

against the United States. General John Frémont, the Union army commander in the area, ordered the slaves of any citizen who aided the rebellion to be freed. An irritated Lincoln told Frémont to withdraw the order. "Liberating slaves of traiterous [sic] owners, will alarm our . . . [slaveholding] friends, and turn them against us," Lincoln warned the general in a letter.[8] Frémont, who supported abolition, sent his wife to Washington to argue that the army should be used against slavery. In a hard voice, Lincoln informed her that it was "a war for a great national idea, the Union, and . . . General Frémont should not have dragged the Negro into it."[9]

Lincoln and the Abolitionists

From the time the fighting began, abolitionists in and out of Congress constantly pressured the president to make the end of slavery a goal of the war. Lincoln's reasons for resisting these demands involved far more than concern about the border states. He knew that most northern whites did not yet support the end of slavery or equality for African Americans. "You . . . overestimate the number in the country who hold such views," Lincoln told one abolitionist. "The great masses of this country care comparatively little about the Negro." Then he added, "When the hour comes for dealing with slavery, I trust I will be willing to do my duty."[10] To a committee of abolitionists who visited the White House in late 1861 to urge Lincoln to attack slavery, he replied:

It would do no good to go ahead any faster than the country would follow. . . . We didn't go into the war to put down slavery, but to put the flag back; and to act any differently at this moment would, I have no doubt, not only weaken our cause, but smack of bad faith; for I should never have had votes enough to send me here, if the people had supposed I should try to use my power to upset slavery. . . . No! we must wait until every other means has been exhausted."[11]

Emancipation and Military Policy

These responses suggest that Lincoln knew he might eventually need to take some drastic action against slavery—not because of antislavery pressures or for moral reasons, but as a way to end the rebellion. As the war continued to go poorly for the Union, the president began to realize how important slavery was to the South's military success.

The Confederate government refused to arm slaves as soldiers. But slaves provided vital aid to southern armies as wagon drivers, cooks, and in other noncombat roles. Every slave who filled such a job freed up a white Southerner to fight. Slaves also continued to do the work on plantations and in the South's few factories that allowed the Confederates to carry out the war. "This rebellion has its source and life in slavery," declared an Indiana congressman in January 1862. "As laborers, if not as soldiers, [the South's slaves] will be the allies of the rebels."[12]

From the beginning of the war, wherever Union armies invaded the South, nearby slaves sought freedom

These slaves were photographed escaping to the protection of the Union army during its invasion of Virginia in July 1862.

by escaping to the Union lines. When slaveholders demanded the return of the escapees, some Union generals refused to comply. These commanders argued that if slaves were "property," as the South had always claimed, then they could be taken from their "owner" like any other item an enemy used to make war.

In August 1861, Congress made this argument the official position of the U.S. government when it passed the Confiscation Act. This law allowed the army to refuse to return any slave who was directly providing labor for the Confederate military. Lincoln did not enforce the law, because he realized that it was a step toward emancipation—a direction in which he was not yet ready to go. So some Union officers, many of whom did not oppose slavery, continued to return captured and escaped slaves to their masters. However, the fact remains that slaves were first set free by actions by congressmen and generals, not by the policies of President Lincoln.

Congress Pushes the President

Hoping to regain leadership on the emancipation issue, Lincoln turned to his long-held solution to slavery— gradual compensated emancipation and colonization. He believed that if the border states adopted this plan, the South would become discouraged and end the war. In December 1861, Lincoln asked Congress to provide money for the purchase of slaves' freedom. He recommended that these freed slaves be colonized outside the United States "in a climate congenial [agreeable] to them."[13]

In March 1862, Lincoln hosted a meeting of border-state congressmen to push his idea. Delaware, the border state where slavery was weakest, had already turned down his proposal to pay slaveholders $400 per slave to end slavery over a five- to thirty-year period. (The value of a field hand at the time was about $1,500.) He was disappointed when the other border states also rejected his proposal.

Meanwhile, Congress continued to move ahead with its own emancipation program. A law passed in March forbade the army from returning any slave to a rebel master. In April, Congress ended slavery in Washington, D.C. Only when Lincoln threatened to not sign this law did Congress agree to pay slaveholders

THIS IS OUR COUNTRY BY BIRTH. . . . WE HAVE AS STRONG AN ATTACHMENT TO [IT] . . . AS ANY OTHER PEOPLE. . . . THIS IS THE COUNTRY OF OUR CHOICE, BEING OUR FATHERS' COUNTRY. . . . WE LOVE THIS LAND AND HAVE CONTRIBUTED OUR SHARE TO ITS PROSPERITY AND WEALTH. . . .

WE HAVE THE RIGHT TO HAVE APPLIED TO OURSELVES THOSE RIGHTS NAMED IN THE DECLARATION OF INDEPENDENCE, . . . SINCE WE HELPED TO GAIN OUR COUNTRY'S INDEPENDENCE, UNDER [GEORGE] WASHINGTON, ON HER BATTLEFIELDS AS WELL AS IN THE CORNFIELDS . . . AND ARE WILLING AND READY EVEN NOW TO FIGHT OUR COUNTRY'S BATTLES AGAINST SLAVEHOLDING TRAITORS AND REBELS. . . . AT THIS VERY TIME, WHEN OUR COUNTRY IS STRUGGLING FOR LIFE, WE ARE CALLED UPON BY THE PRESIDENT OF THE UNITED STATES TO LEAVE THIS LAND AND GO TO ANOTHER COUNTRY, TO CARRY OUT HIS FAVORITE SCHEME OF COLONIZATION. BUT AT THIS CRISIS, WE FEEL DISPOSED TO REFUSE THE OFFERS OF THE PRESIDENT. . . .

WE COLORED PEOPLE ARE ALL LOYAL MEN, WHICH IS MORE THAN ANY OTHER CLASS OF PEOPLE IN THE COUNTRY CAN SAY. THERE ARE . . . NO COLORED REBELS. . . . IF WE ARE PERMITTED TO FIGHT OUR COUNTRY'S BATTLES AND AN ARMY OF COLORED MEN WERE PERMITTED TO MARCH INTO THOSE REBEL STATES, . . . THE REBELS WOULD SUFFER FROM OUR PRESENCE.

In August 1862, a mass meeting of African Americans on Long Island, New York, prepared this response to Lincoln's proposals that freed slaves be colonized outside the United States.

$300 per slave and provide funds to colonize the freed African Americans. In June it abolished slavery in the territories. This time no compensation was paid to the slaveholders.

Then, in mid-July, Congress made an even bolder move against slavery by passing the Second Confiscation Act. This act declared that after sixty days, all slaves of rebel slaveholders would be free. Union armies would have to conquer the South before the law could be enforced, of course. But Congress had taken the very step that abolitionists had long asked of Lincoln—to free the South's slaves and make the war a conflict over slavery. More than any other action, this law pushed the president to issue the Emancipation Proclamation.

Moving Toward Emancipation

No one knows exactly when Lincoln first began to seriously consider acting against slavery. Most historians believe the evidence points to the late spring or early summer of 1862. By then, events in Europe, on the battlefield, and in the North, made such action seem both possible and necessary.

When the Civil War began, Lincoln had used the U.S. Navy to blockade the South's seaports. The blockade cut off the South's trade with Great Britain, which depended on southern cotton for its textile mills. This loss caused nearly a half million British textile workers to be laid off their jobs. Some of Lincoln's advisors began to fear that Britain might come to the South's aid in the war.

Great Britain declared itself officially neutral when the Civil War began. Although the British people were strongly against slavery, the South's ties with Britain were old and deep. Many British government leaders openly favored Confederate independence. Americans in Europe advised Lincoln that only three events could keep Britain from interfering in the war: a major Union victory, the capture of a southern port and the release of cotton to British factories, or the announcement of a policy to free the slaves.

Neither the first nor the second of these events seemed likely. Southern forces continued to defeat Union armies. In late June 1862, an advance on Richmond, Virginia, that had begun in March was finally turned back by the Confederates. Union troops suffered thousands of casualties during this campaign.

Such loss of life had a great effect in the North. Many Northerners began to question whether merely saving the Union was worth the terrible human cost of the war. Increasingly, they began to demand that the rebels pay for this suffering by forfeiting their slaves.

The high number of casualties also dried up the supply of men needed for Union armies. In early July, Lincoln called for 300,000 more volunteers. Fewer than 50,000 responded. The governor of Massachusetts told the president to not expect a better result as long as he continued fighting a war that left slavery intact.

Still Lincoln hesitated. When Senator Charles Sumner, a leading abolitionist, suggested that July 4—

This 1862 cartoon shows Northern fears that Britain's need for cotton would overcome their dislike of slavery and cause them to aid the South in the war.

Independence Day—would be a good time for a proclamation of emancipation, the president replied, "I would do it if I were not afraid that half the officers [in the army] would fling down their arms and three more states [Kentucky, Maryland, and Missouri] would rise [rebel]."[14]

Lincoln Makes His Decision

On July 12, Lincoln again appealed to border-state leaders to support his plan for gradual compensated emancipation. Congress was then considering passage of the Second Confiscation Act. The president believed that if it passed, the movement for emancipation could probably not be stopped. He warned that if slaveholders passed up the chance to be paid for freeing slaves, they might someday be forced to do it for no compensation.[15]

When this final appeal was rejected, Lincoln felt free to act. On July 13, he advised Secretary of State William Seward and Secretary of the Navy Gideon Welles that he was going to issue an emancipation proclamation. The president observed that slavery strengthened the South's ability to make war. The slaves' emancipation was "a military necessity, absolutely essential to the preservation of the Union," Lincoln concluded. "We must free the slaves or be ourselves subdued. . . . The Administration must set an example and strike at the heart of the rebellion."[16]

On July 17, a displeased president reluctantly approved the Second Confiscation Act. Congress now controlled emancipation, even though Lincoln questioned its constitutional right to do so. "It is startling to say that congress can free a slave within a state," he observed before signing the law.[17]

Five days later, the president presented a proposed emancipation proclamation to his cabinet. The short document was a clear attempt by Lincoln to regain from Congress control over the emancipation issue. It first called attention to section six of the Second Confiscation Act—the section that declared the rebels' slaves to be free. Next Lincoln's proposed proclamation cleverly made Southerners aware that they could avoid this law—and the loss of their slaves—by ending their rebellion:

> I, Abraham Lincoln, President of the United States, do hereby . . . warn all persons [covered by] said sixth section to cease participating in . . . the existing rebellion . . . and to return to their proper allegiance to the United States, on pain of the forfeitures and seizures . . . by said sixth section provided.[18]

Charles Sumner, a supporter of political rights for African Americans, led those Republicans in the Senate who wanted an immediate end to slavery.

Then the document went on to announce Lincoln's intent to establish a program for the "gradual abolishment of slavery" which any state "recognizing . . . the authority of the United States . . . may voluntarily adopt." Finally, Lincoln's proposed proclamation reaffirmed that the war was being fought to restore the nation, and *not* to end slavery. It concluded by stating that as a "necessary military measure" to accomplish this goal, Lincoln *would* free the slaves in any state that was still in rebellion against the United States on January 1, 1863.

After months of resistance and hesitation, Lincoln now wanted to issue his proclamation immediately. But cabinet members reminded the president of how badly the war was going. They advised him that his announcement would have a greater effect if it followed a battlefield success.

Another Union army was set to invade Virginia in early August. Its commander, General John Pope, was confident that he would defeat the rebels. Lincoln decided to delay his proclamation until Pope provided the needed victory.

6

THE DAWN OF FREEDOM

During August 1862, President Lincoln anxiously followed the progress of General Pope and his army as it advanced into Virginia. His July proclamation remained in his desk, awaiting a Union victory on the battlefield. "From time to time I added or changed a line, touching it up here and there," Lincoln recalled later.[1] Finally, in late August, the dreadful news arrived. The Confederates had attacked Pope's troops at Bull Run, the site of the war's first major battle the previous summer. The results of the second battle were like the first. The Union army was badly beaten. A dejected president shared the news with his secretary, John Hay: "Well, John, we are whipped again, I am afraid."[2] His proclamation of emancipation would have wait a while longer.

Seeking a Sign

Pope's defeat at the Second Battle of Bull Run threw the president into a deep depression. He began to question his emancipation policy and even the war itself. "In great contests each party claims to act in accordance with the will of God," he wrote. "God cannot be *for*, and *against* the same thing at the same time."[3]

Several days later a group of religious leaders arrived from Chicago to pressure Lincoln for a proclamation of emancipation. His response shows that he remained unsure this was the course to follow:

> I am approached with the . . . opposite opinions and advice . . . by religious men, who are equally certain that they represent the Divine will. . . . If it is probable that God would reveal his will to others on a point so connected with my duty, it might be supposed he would reveal it directly to me. . . . It is my earnest desire to know the will of Providence in this matter. . . . Whatever shall appear to be God's will I will do.[4]

As Confederate troops invaded Maryland, he looked for a sign that would tell him whether emancipation was God's will. On the day that Lincoln replied to the Chicago ministers, the Union soldier found General Lee's invasion plans. Lincoln swore to God that if the Union won the coming battle, he would issue the Emancipation Proclamation.

The Battle of Antietam on September 17, 1862, was not the overwhelming victory Lincoln hoped for. However, he accepted it as the sign he was seeking. The president called a meeting of his cabinet for the next Monday. Over the weekend he made some final changes to the proclamation he had been working on since July.

On Monday, September 22, Lincoln presented his proclamation to his cabinet. "I have got you together to hear what I have written down. I do not wish your advice about the main matter—for that I have determined for myself," he explained. "If there is anything in the expressions I use, or in any other minor matter, which anyone of you thinks had best be changed, I shall be glad to receive the suggestions."[5] But before he began to read his proclamation, he showed his continued doubts. "I must do the best I can," he said, "and bear the responsibility of taking the course which I feel I ought to take."[6]

Lincoln's uncertainty still lingered the next day, when supporters gathered outside the White House to celebrate his action. "I can only trust in God I have made no mistake," he told the crowd. "It is now for the country and the world to pass judgment on it."[7]

The Preliminary Proclamation

The proclamation that Lincoln issued on September 22 is known as the Preliminary Emancipation Proclamation. It announced the president's intent to grant freedom on January 1, 1863, to "all persons held as slaves within any state, or designated part of a state, the people whereof shall then be in rebellion against the United States."[8] It further stated that on January 1, Lincoln would issue the final Emancipation Proclamation and name the states, or parts of states, to which it applied.

Of course, this wording left open the possibility that a Confederate state could avoid the end of slavery by quitting the war and returning to the Union before

January 1. Although no one really expected that to happen, it was an outcome Lincoln was clearly willing to accept. He had written Horace Greeley on this subject just a month before. At that time he had told Greeley his purpose was to reunite the nation, whether it required the freeing of some slaves, of all slaves, or of no slaves.

Another passage in the Preliminary Emancipation Proclamation also shows that Lincoln was willing to allow slavery to continue in order to reunite the nation:

> It is my purpose, upon the next meeting of Congress to again recommend the adoption of a practical measure tendering [offering] pecuniary [financial] aid to the free acceptance or rejection of all slave-states, so called, the people whereof may not then be in rebellion against the United States, and which states, may then have voluntarily adopted, or thereafter may voluntarily adopt, immediate, or gradual abolishment of slavery.[9]

Here Lincoln was offering his idea of compensated emancipation to slave states that returned to the Union. But even this program would be voluntary. Each slave state would be free to accept it, or to turn it down and maintain slavery. The only states to which the Emancipation Proclamation would apply were those that continued to rebel. This would happen only if United States forces were able conquer them and force them back into the Union.

LINCOLN'S LAST WARNING

"Now if you don't come down, I'll cut the tree from under you."

This cartoon appeared in Harper's Weekly *magazine soon after the Preliminary Emancipation Proclamation was issued. It shows Lincoln threatening to destroy slavery if the South does not end its rebellion.*

Reactions in the North and South

Government employees worked late into the night to print thousands of copies of the president's Preliminary Emancipation Proclamation. Copies were sent to American newspapers and to nations throughout the world. Some 15,000 copies were sent to army commanders to share with their troops. Within a week, it was the main topic of discussion in the North and South, and in their armies.

As might be expected, Lincoln's announcement was harshly condemned throughout the South and in the Confederate army. Many white Southerners saw it as an attempt by Lincoln to stir up a slave revolt. They pointed to the preliminary proclamation as yet another reason to keep on fighting.

Many slaves soon heard of Lincoln's proclamation, too. As it appeared in southern newspapers, the few slaves who could read shared its contents with others. In addition, some white Southerners talked about the proclamation without noticing that slaves were listening. These slaves also spread the news. But many slaves' lives became more difficult because of the proclamation. Fearing that it would encourage escapes or revolts, white Southerners tightened their control over slavery.

In the North, public opinion at first seemed to support Lincoln's announcement. "The grandest proclamation ever issued by man," reported the Chicago *Tribune*. "God bless Abraham Lincoln," proclaimed Greeley's *New York Tribune*.[10] A Cincinnati newspaper was delighted that Lincoln was no longer willing to protect "the compulsory [forced] labor system *which feeds the enemy.*"[11] In every major city in the North, huge rallies, parades, and patriotic speeches celebrated the proclamation. Abolitionist William Lloyd Garrison called it "an act of immense historical consequence."[12]

In the Union army, reaction to the proclamation was mixed. Some men in the 1st Minnesota Infantry rioted when they heard the news. For a time, the 109th Illinois regiment refused to fight. But most troops looked on emancipation according to how they thought it would affect the war. Soldiers who believed it would shorten the war tended to favor it. Those who felt it would make the South fight harder generally opposed it. The overall view was probably best summed up by a colonel from Indiana. Few soldiers were abolitionists, he observed, but "there is a desire to destroy everything that . . . gives the rebels strength."[13] A corporal from Pennsylvania agreed. "If slavery aids the rebellion it will have to go," he wrote. "This is what has given them power in times past. It is slave labor that feeds their Army."[14]

Reactions from Overseas

Both Britain and France worried that Lincoln's action would inspire a general slave uprising in the South. This concern was due to wording in the preliminary proclamation that "the military . . . will do no act . . . to repress such persons [slaves] . . . in any efforts they may make for their actual freedom."[15] This language was widely

New York newspaper editor and abolitionist Horace Greeley used his paper to demand that Lincoln make the end of slavery a Union goal in the Civil War.

viewed in Europe, and in the South, as an invitation to slaves to begin a bloody revolt.

Another worry was that Lincoln's action would prolong the war rather than shorten it. This would lengthen the time British and French textile mills would remain without southern cotton. An American official in France reported to Lincoln that the French government was more interested in ending the war by the next cotton harvest than it was in emancipation.

Britain's prime minister, Henry John Palmerson, the head of its government, called the proclamation "trash."[16] Another top British official suggested the time had come to consider the South an independent nation. Lincoln moved quickly to counter these reactions. He knew that despite their government's position, the British people were strongly against slavery. So he secretly sent money to pay for public rallies there in support of the Union and emancipation. He also wrote letters to groups of British workers. In these letters he blamed the loss of southern cotton not on the Union Navy's blockade of southern ports, but on the South itself for continuing the war.

Not until much later was it known how close Britain and France actually came to helping the South win independence by the fall of 1862. In order to restore the flow of southern cotton to Europe, French ruler Louis Napoleon suggested to British leaders that the two countries pressure Lincoln to stop the war. Key British leaders favored this plan. Only after an angry debate in the British cabinet, in which officials who supported the Union pointed to Lincoln's proclamation, was the idea rejected.

A Critical Hundred Days

One well-known historian has called the hundred days between the preliminary proclamation and the final proclamation the most difficult period of Lincoln's presidency.[17] As the early excitement died down in the North, strong voices of opposition to the proclamation began to be heard. Many attacked the proclamation as an illegal and unconstitutional act that exceeded the president's powers. Others predicted that it would prolong the war. Democrats made the proclamation an issue in the congressional elections of November 1862. Although Republicans remained in control of Congress, the Democrats made huge gains. *The New York Times* called the results a rejection of the president's policies on the war and slavery.[18]

Even many supporters of emancipation became less enthusiastic as they gave the preliminary proclamation a closer look. Garrison, for example, criticized it for allowing slavery to continue in places under Union control. Others noted that it freed the slaves only in places where Lincoln had no ability to do so.

As January 1 approached, rumors spread that opposition at home and overseas would cause Lincoln to not issue the final proclamation. On Christmas Eve, Charles Sumner visited the White House to find out if the rumors were true. Lincoln assured him they were not. The army had suffered a terrible defeat at the Battle of Fredericksburg just eleven days before. This failure of yet another invasion of Virginia made Lincoln even more convinced of the need to go ahead with his plan. "My mind is made up," the president said. "*It must be done*." "Hallelujah," Sumner replied. But other northern leaders were not pleased at this news. "There is no hope," complained Illinois senator Orville Browning. "The Proclamation will come."[19]

Issuing the Emancipation Proclamation

On January 1, 1863, Lincoln rose early to put the final touches on his Emancipation Proclamation. Then he went downstairs to host the traditional New Year's

The strain of the Civil War showed on Lincoln's face in this photo, taken at about the time he issued the Emancipation Proclamation.

Day reception at the White House. By mid-afternoon all the guests had left, and the president returned to his study upstairs to sign the proclamation.

There was no ceremony. Only a few people were present. Lincoln's arm was so sore from shaking hundreds of hands at the reception that he had trouble signing his name. "If my hand trembles when I sign the Proclamation, all who examine the document hereafter will say, 'He hesitated,'" Lincoln complained.[20] Then he noted that "I never, in my life, felt more certain that I was doing right than I do in signing this paper."[21]

In the final Emancipation Proclamation, Lincoln dealt with many of the objections raised to the preliminary proclamation. All mention of voluntary compensated emancipation and colonization was gone from the final proclamation. In addition, it addressed the concerns that Lincoln was encouraging a slave rebellion. The final Emancipation Proclamation called on all slaves it declared to be free "to abstain from [avoid] all violence, unless in necessary self-defense."

Lincoln also focused on the objection that he did not have the legal authority to free slaves. Article II, Section 1 of the Constitution makes the president "Commander in Chief of the Army and Navy of the United States." Lincoln considered emancipation to be among the weapons of war that a president, as commander in chief, possessed. It was on this basis that the Emancipation Proclamation granted freedom to the rebels' slaves:

> I, Abraham Lincoln, President of the United States, by virtue of the power in me vested as Commander-In-Chief, of the Army and Navy of the United States in time of actual armed rebellion against authority and government of the United States, and as a fit and necessary war measure for suppressing said rebellion. . . .

Lincoln reemphasized this authority at the end of the proclamation by referring to emancipation as "warranted by the Constitution, upon military necessity." But this clever interpretation of the Constitution did not really solve the legal problems the proclamation raised.

As promised in the preliminary proclamation, the Emancipation Proclamation listed the "States and parts of States" that were in rebellion. Tennessee was omitted, even though Union forces only controlled the western third of the state. The proclamation also named seven counties in Virginia and thirteen parishes in Louisiana that the Union controlled and where emancipation did not apply. (In Louisiana counties are called parishes.)

Also not included in the Emancipation Proclamation were fifty counties in northwest Virginia. Few people in this part of Virginia held slaves. Most of these counties had split from Virginia at the start of the war. In June 1863, they all were admitted to the Union as the state of West Virginia. The new state's constitution immediately freed all children born to slaves after July 4, 1863, and all existing children of slaves when they reached age twenty-five.

BY THE PRESIDENT OF THE UNITED STATES OF AMERICA:

A PROCLAMATION

WHEREAS ON THE 22ND DAY OF SEPTEMBER, A.D. 1862, A PROCLAMATION WAS ISSUED BY THE PRESIDENT OF THE UNITED STATES, CONTAINING, AMONG OTHER THINGS, THE FOLLOWING, TO WIT:

"THAT ON THE 1ST DAY OF JANUARY, A.D. 1863, ALL PERSONS HELD AS SLAVES WITHIN ANY STATE OR DESIGNATED PART OF A STATE THE PEOPLE WHEREOF SHALL THEN BE IN REBELLION AGAINST THE UNITED STATES SHALL BE THEN, THENCEFORWARD, AND FOREVER FREE; AND THE EXECUTIVE GOVERNMENT OF THE UNITED STATES, INCLUDING THE MILITARY AND NAVAL AUTHORITY THEREOF, WILL RECOGNIZE AND MAINTAIN THE FREEDOM OF SUCH PERSONS AND WILL DO NO ACT OR ACTS TO REPRESS SUCH PERSONS, OR ANY OF THEM, IN ANY EFFORTS THEY MAY MAKE FOR THEIR ACTUAL FREEDOM.

"THAT THE EXECUTIVE WILL ON THE 1ST DAY OF JANUARY AFORESAID, BY PROCLAMATION, DESIGNATE THE STATES AND PARTS OF STATES, IF ANY, IN WHICH THE PEOPLE THEREOF, RESPECTIVELY, SHALL THEN BE IN REBELLION AGAINST THE UNITED STATES; AND THE FACT THAT ANY STATE OR THE PEOPLE THEREOF SHALL ON THAT DAY BE IN GOOD FAITH REPRESENTED IN THE CONGRESS OF THE UNITED STATES BY MEMBERS CHOSEN THERETO AT ELECTIONS WHEREIN A MAJORITY OF THE QUALIFIED VOTERS OF SUCH STATES SHALL

(continues)

The second and third paragraphs of the Emancipation Proclamation, issued on January 1, 1863, quote the major parts of Lincoln's Preliminary Emancipation Proclamation of September 22, 1862.

HAVE PARTICIPATED SHALL, IN THE ABSENCE OF STRONG COUNTERVAILING TESTIMONY, BE DEEMED CONCLUSIVE EVIDENCE THAT SUCH STATE AND THE PEOPLE THEREOF ARE NOT THEN IN REBELLION AGAINST THE UNITED STATES."

NOW, THEREFORE, I, ABRAHAM LINCOLN, PRESIDENT OF THE UNITED STATES, BY VIRTUE OF THE POWER IN ME VESTED AS COMMANDER-IN-CHIEF OF THE ARMY AND NAVY OF THE UNITED STATES IN TIME OF ACTUAL ARMED REBELLION AGAINST THE AUTHORITY AND GOVERNMENT OF THE UNITED STATES, AND AS A FIT AND NECESSARY WAR MEASURE FOR SUPPRESSING SAID REBELLION, DO, ON THIS 1ST DAY OF JANUARY, A.D. 1863, AND IN ACCORDANCE WITH MY PURPOSE SO TO DO, PUBLICLY PROCLAIMED FOR THE FULL PERIOD OF ONE HUNDRED DAYS FROM THE FIRST DAY ABOVE MENTIONED, ORDER AND DESIGNATE AS THE STATES AND PARTS OF STATES WHEREIN THE PEOPLE THEREOF, RESPECTIVELY, ARE THIS DAY IN REBELLION AGAINST THE UNITED STATES THE FOLLOWING, TO WIT:

ARKANSAS, TEXAS, LOUISIANA (EXCEPT THE PARISHES OF ST. BERNARD, PALQUEMINES, JEFFERSON, ST. JOHN, ST. CHARLES, ST. JAMES, ASCENSION, ASSUMPTION, TERREBONE, LAFOURCHE, ST. MARY, ST. MARTIN, AND ORLEANS, INCLUDING THE CITY OF NEW ORLEANS), MISSISSIPPI, ALABAMA, FLORIDA, GEORGIA, SOUTH CAROLINA, NORTH CAROLINA, AND VIRGINIA (EXCEPT THE FORTY-EIGHT COUNTIES DESIGNATED AS WEST VIRGINIA, AND ALSO THE COUNTIES OF BERKELEY, ACCOMAC, MORTHHAMPTON, ELIZABETH CITY, YORK, PRINCESS ANNE, AND NORFOLK, INCLUDING THE CITIES OF NORFOLK AND PORTSMOUTH), AND WHICH EXCEPTED PARTS ARE FOR THE PRESENT LEFT PRECISELY AS IF THIS PROCLAMATION WERE NOT ISSUED.

(continues)

AND BY VIRTUE OF THE POWER AND FOR THE PURPOSE AFORESAID, I DO ORDER AND DECLARE THAT ALL PERSONS HELD AS SLAVES WITHIN SAID DESIGNATED STATES AND PARTS OF STATES ARE, AND HENCEFORWARD SHALL BE, FREE; AND THAT THE EXECUTIVE GOVERNMENT OF THE UNITED STATES, INCLUDING THE MILITARY AND NAVAL AUTHORITIES THEREOF, WILL RECOGNIZE AND MAINTAIN THE FREEDOM OF SAID PERSONS.

AND I HEREBY ENJOIN UPON THE PEOPLE SO DECLARED TO BE FREE TO ABSTAIN FROM ALL VIOLENCE, UNLESS IN NECESSARY SELF-DEFENCE; AND I RECOMMEND TO THEM THAT, IN ALL CASE WHEN ALLOWED, THEY LABOR FAITHFULLY FOR REASONABLE WAGES.

AND I FURTHER DECLARE AND MAKE KNOWN THAT SUCH PERSONS OF SUITABLE CONDITION WILL BE RECEIVED INTO THE ARMED SERVICE OF THE UNITED STATES TO GARRISON FORTS, POSITIONS, STATIONS, AND OTHER PLACES, AND TO MAN VESSELS OF ALL SORTS IN SAID SERVICE.

AND UPON THIS ACT, SINCERELY BELIEVED TO BE AN ACT OF JUSTICE, WARRANTED BY THE CONSTITUTION UPON MILITARY NECESSITY, I INVOKE THE CONSIDERATE JUDGMENT OF MANKIND AND THE GRACIOUS FAVOR OF ALMIGHTY GOD.

IN WITNESS WHEREOF, I HAVE HEREUNTO SET MY HAND, AND CAUSED THE SEAL OF THE UNITED STATES TO BE AFFIXED.

DONE IN THE CITY OF WASHINGTON, THIS FIRST DAY OF JANUARY, IN THE YEAR OF OUR LORD ONE THOUSAND EIGHT HUNDRED AND SIXTY-THREE, AND OF THE INDEPENDENCE OF THE UNITED STATES OF AMERICA THE EIGHTY-SEVENTH.

ABRAHAM LINCOLN

Reactions to Emancipation

Emancipation Day signaled another series of celebrations across the North. But few opinions had changed during the hundred days between the preliminary proclamation and the final Emancipation Proclamation. If anything, opposition became stronger than ever.

The strongest opposition came from the Midwest, where the abolition movement was weakest. Like Lincoln himself, many whites in the rural southern parts of Ohio, Indiana, and Illinois had family ties with the South. They supported the Union, but they were not great foes of slavery. Even those who, like Lincoln, had opposed its spread, did not object to slavery continuing where it already existed. Many feared that slaves freed from southern plantations would come into their region and compete with them as farmers and farm laborers.

Having lived in southern Indiana and southern Illinois, Lincoln understood such attitudes and concerns. This was likely why he had long supported voluntary emancipation and the colonization of freed slaves outside the United States. But most abolitionists had opposed the voluntary emancipation program set forth in the preliminary proclamation, and northern African Americans strongly opposed colonization. So Lincoln had dropped both ideas from his final proclamation.

To many Northerners the final Emancipation Proclamation seemed to drastically alter the goals of the war. After January 1, rebels could not save slavery by

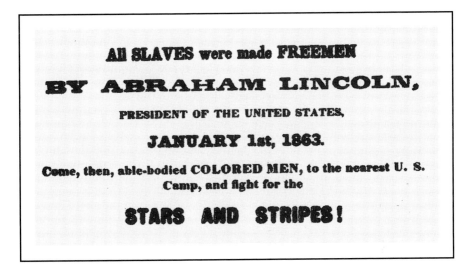

All SLAVES were made FREEMEN
BY ABRAHAM LINCOLN,
PRESIDENT OF THE UNITED STATES,
JANUARY 1st, 1863.
Come, then, able-bodied COLORED MEN, to the nearest U. S. Camp, and fight for the
STARS AND STRIPES!

This recruiting poster called on black men in the South to volunteer to fight in the Union armies following the Emancipation Proclamation.

giving up and rejoining the Union. Nor would they have the choice of gradual, voluntary emancipation. So they had no reason to stop fighting. Thus, to many Northerners Lincoln's action appeared to make the war a fight more to end slavery than to restore the Union.

Other critics complained that the Emancipation Proclamation did not really accomplish anything. The *New York World* newspaper reported:

> Immediate practical effect, it has none; the slaves remaining in precisely the same condition as before. They still live on the plantations, tenant [live in] their accustomed hovels [miserable houses], obey the command of their master . . . doing the work he requires precisely as though Mr. Lincoln had not declared them free.[22]

Abolitionists recognized these limitations, too. But most supported the Emancipation Proclamation as the first step toward an end to slavery, which they now believed would surely come. Charlotte Forten, a black abolitionist from Philadelphia, shared this view. Writing to a friend on January 1, she proclaimed: "What a grand, glorious day this has been. The dawn of freedom which it heralds may not break upon us at once; but it will surely come, and sooner, I believe, than we have ever dared hope before. My soul is glad with an exceeding great gladness."[23]

The Proclamation's Effects on the War

Opposition to the war existed in the North from the time the fighting began. But unhappiness over the Emancipation Proclamation helped a strong peace movement to develop in the Midwest in 1863 and 1864. Public rallies and parades protested changing the war into an abolition crusade and called for an end to the fighting. Opponents encouraged Union soldiers to desert rather than fight to free slaves.

Many Midwesterners in the army agreed. "This is a negro war," complained an Ohio lieutenant. "If I had known, I would never have joined." "I did not [join the army to] fight for Emancipation," an Illinois captain wrote. "I hope to sink in hell if I ever draw my sword to fight for the negroes."[24] So many soldiers from two southern Illinois regiments deserted that the regiments had to be disbanded.

African American soldiers served in all-black units that were commanded by white officers. These soldiers are from Company E of the 4th U.S. Colored Infantry.

In early 1863, the Illinois legislature demanded that Lincoln withdraw the Emancipation Proclamation and make peace with the South. When it tried to pass laws that interfered with Lincoln's war policies, the governor broke it up and ruled the state alone. Lincoln sent troops to Illinois to help keep the peace. A similar situation occurred in Indiana. The governor there governed without a legislature for two years after it too tried to block the state's participation in the war.

However, despite the troublesome opposition to it, the Emancipation Proclamation had some major effects on the Civil War. One of these, already noted, is that it prevented Britain and France from forcing a settlement of the war that would grant the South independence. The Confederates themselves recognized this shift in overseas opinion. After January 1863, the South's representatives in Britain changed their strategy. Confederate leaders told them to propose that the South would free its slaves if they thought this proposal could restore British support for southern independence.

Of course, despite the criticism that it accomplished nothing, the Emancipation Proclamation *did* free slaves in areas of the South that Union forces conquered after January 1863. In mid-1863, the course of the war began to change. As Union forces wore down Confederate armies, Lincoln's troops started winning victories. One Union soldier reported the proclamation's effect as his army moved through Georgia in 1864.

> Every day, as we marched on we could see, on each side of our line of march, crowds of these people [slaves] coming to us through roads and across the fields, bringing with them all their earthly goods. . . . They were allowed to follow in rear of our column, and at times they were almost equal in numbers to the army they were following.[25]

This scene was repeated throughout the South, wherever Union forces gained control. By July 1864, General Ulysses S. Grant's army in Mississippi and Tennessee had attracted more than 113,000 "freedmen," the term applied to former slaves. Some had been released from slavery by their masters as the army approached. Others had simply run away. Grant hired many of these freedmen as cooks, barbers, wagon drivers, and other laborers to serve his army. Others joined the army itself. Other freedmen served in the same way in parts of Virginia and North Carolina where Union armies gained control.

Emancipation and Black Soldiers

One of the Emancipation Proclamation's most important effects was that it encouraged African Americans to join the fight to end slavery. "Such persons of suitable condition will be received into the armed service of the United States," Lincoln wrote in his proclamation.

Enlisting African Americans into the army was not Lincoln's idea. Abolitionists, some Republican officials, and northern black leaders had been urging it for months. In 1862, Congress passed a law that allowed African Americans to serve in the military. But Northern troops in the Civil War were raised by state governments. Like Lincoln, most northern state leaders showed little interest in recruiting black troops. They did not believe that African Americans would be effective soldiers.

Even when he issued his preliminary proclamation, Lincoln had remained opposed to using black troops to fight the war. During the hundred days between the preliminary and final proclamations, however, Lincoln was continuously pressured by Senator Sumner and others to encourage African-American volunteers. "I suppose the time has come," he replied as he prepared the final Emancipation Proclamation.[26]

By the spring of 1863, Lincoln's views had changed completely, and he urged a huge effort to recruit black troops. "The colored population is the great *available* and yet *unavailed* of [unused] force for restoring the Union," the president observed.[27] Black leaders played a major role in urging African Americans to join the fight. "Liberty won by white men would lose half its luster," Frederick Douglass claimed in an appeal to the black population of New York.[28]

Despite the fact they began to serve only in 1863, some 180,000 African Americans had enlisted in Union armies by the war's end in May 1865. About half were slaves freed in the southern states. All-black regiments fought in about forty major battles of the war. And more than 37,000 black soldiers gave their lives for the Union and the cause of freedom.

Lincoln pointed to this loyal service to shame white Northerners who opposed his Emancipation Proclamation. In a statement that was read at a huge war protest rally in Springfield, Illinois, in September 1863, the president made the following observation:

> You say you will not fight to free negroes. Some of them seem willing to fight for you. . . . [When this war is over] there will be some black men who can remember that, with silent tongue . . . and well-poised bayonet, they have helped mankind on to this great consummation [victory]; while, I fear, there will be some white ones, unable to forget that . . . they have strove to hinder [block] it.[29]

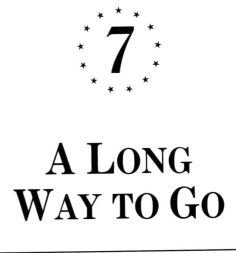

Among the reasons African Americans volunteered in such large numbers to fight in the bloody Civil War was a very practical one. Frederick Douglass summed up why his people were so eager to wear the uniform of the U.S. Army:

A LONG WAY TO GO

> Once let the black man get upon his person the brass letters U.S.; let him get an eagle on his button, and a musket on his shoulder, and bullets in his pocket, and there is no power on the earth . . . which can deny that he has earned the right of citizenship in the United States.[1]

But Douglass was overly optimistic when he made this prediction in August 1863. There was no guarantee that freedmen or even free black Northerners would become U.S. citizens after the war. In fact, serious questions existed about whether slaves freed by the Emancipation Proclamation were legally free.

Legal Issues with the Emancipation Proclamation

The critics who charged that the Emancipation Proclamation was unconstitutional stood on solid legal ground. Since the nation's beginning, in states where slavery had been abolished, it had always been done by changing the state constitution or by passing a state law. The federal government had never before interfered with the practice of slavery inside a state. Many, if not most, Americans believed that neither Congress nor the president had the right to do so.

Lincoln issued the Emancipation Proclamation using his wartime powers as head of the armed forces. But under international law, property seized from civilians during a war must be returned, or the owners paid for their loss when the war is over. Did this mean that freedmen could be required to return to slavery when the war ended? What about people who had not been freed during the war and remained enslaved in the South? The great majority of slaves fell into this category. Would emancipation apply to them too? These and other troubling legal questions arose in the months following the proclamation.

Many abolitionists feared the Supreme Court would declare the Emancipation Proclamation unconstitutional after the war. Even Lincoln himself questioned whether it was truly legal. Months after issuing it he privately admitted this concern: "I felt that measures, otherwise unconstitutional, might become lawful, by becoming indispensable [necessary] to . . . the preservation of the nation. Right or wrong, I assumed this ground. . . ."[2]

Another problem was slavery in parts of the South exempted from the proclamation because they were in Union hands when it took effect. Related to this was the issue of slavery in the border states. As the war shifted in the Union's favor, concern lessened that these states might join the Confederacy. So pressure increased to end slavery in these places, too. But Lincoln doubted the Emancipation Proclamation could ever apply to areas not included in it: "The original proclamation has no constitutional or legal justification, except as a military measure. . . . If I take the step [of extending it] . . . would I not thus give up all footing upon constitution or law? . . . Could this pass unnoticed, or unresisted?"[3]

The simplest solution to all these issues was for Congress to pass the laws needed to address them. Lincoln opposed this approach because the Supreme Court could declare such laws unconstitutional, too. The border states and defeated southern states might be convinced to each pass the necessary state laws. But that would have been difficult to achieve. Instead, Lincoln supported amending the Constitution. Only three-fourths of the states must approve a proposed amendment for it to apply to all. Also, an amendment cannot be overturned by the Supreme Court.

Emancipation and the Thirteenth Amendment

Lincoln actually attempted to deal with the legal issues surrounding the Emancipation Proclamation before he even issued it. In December 1862, he asked Congress for a constitutional amendment that would protect slaves

In addition to being a timid commander, General George McClellan opposed Lincoln on nearly every war-related issue. After the Battle of Antietam, he resigned from the army and worked openly against Lincoln's policies.

freed by the war and would pay states to free the remainder by 1900. But Congress never acted on this proposal.

In April 1864, an amendment to abolish slavery throughout the United States passed the Senate. But it failed in the House of Representatives. House approval proved difficult for several reasons. Remember that Democrats had made huge gains in the congressional elections in 1862, due largely to voters' unhappiness over Lincoln's Preliminary Emancipation Proclamation. Those gains now kept the Thirteenth Amendment from getting the two-thirds majority needed to send a proposed amendment on to the states for approval.

Opposition to emancipation was only part of the problem. The Constitution had not been amended for sixty years. In addition, all twelve previous amendments either protected people's existing rights or changed the way government worked. The Thirteenth Amendment was the first one to change society itself. It was difficult to convince legislators that the Constitution should be used to achieve a major social reform.

Lincoln's election to a second term as president in November 1864, turned the tide. The Democrats' candidate, General George McClellan, had long opposed emancipation. In Lincoln's eyes his victory over McClellan signaled a shift of public opinion about emancipation. He asked for another House vote on the proposed amendment and pressured congressmen to support it. Largely because of Lincoln's tireless efforts, the Thirteenth Amendment passed the House in January 1865. By December, enough states had approved it to make it part of the Constitution:

> Neither slavery nor involuntary servitude, except as punishment for crime whereof the party shall have been duly convicted, shall exist within the United States, or any place subject to their jurisdiction.

The following year Congress also settled the question of whether freedmen and other African Americans were citizens by passing the Fourteenth Amendment:

> All persons born or naturalized in the United States, and subject to the jurisdiction thereof, are citizens of the United States and of the State wherein they reside.

This amendment was approved by the required number of states and added to the Constitution in 1868. Two years later the Fifteenth Amendment guaranteed that the right to vote could not be denied "on account of race, color, or previous condition of servitude."

The End of the War and Lincoln's Assassination

Another objection to the Emancipation Proclamation was that it would make the South fight harder and thereby prolong the war. Opinions differ over whether this fear came true. Slave labor grew the food that southern soldiers ate. Slaves worked in the shops and factories whose products supplied the Confederate armies. Lincoln estimated that about 200,000 slaves gained their freedom because of the Emancipation Proclamation.[4] This was only a fraction of the four million slaves held in the South. But certainly the loss of 200,000 workers hurt the South's ability to continue fighting.

On the other hand, after the South began to lose battles, Confederate leaders might have surrendered if emancipation had not been an issue. In July 1864, Horace Greeley represented the president at a meeting Confederate officials sought in Niagara Falls, Canada. In February 1865, Lincoln himself met with Confederate vice president Alexander Stephens at Hampton Roads, in a Union-controlled part of Virginia. In both cases, peace talks went nowhere. In part, this was because Lincoln refused to withdraw the Emancipation Proclamation.

John Wilkes Booth hoped to save the South by a spectacular act against the president. When his plot to kidnap Lincoln failed, he turned to assassination. He escaped to Virginia after the shooting, where he was tracked down and killed.

Not until May 1865, after all Confederate armies were defeated or surrendered, did the Civil War come to an end. Lincoln, however, would not live to witness this event. On the night of April 14, 1865, he was shot by Maryland-born actor John Wilkes Booth while attending a play in Washington, D.C. The president died early the next morning. In a sealed letter Booth left to be opened after his death, he indicated that hatred of the Emancipation Proclamation was behind his terrible deed:

> This country was formed for the *white*, not for the black man. And, looking upon *African slavery* from the same standpoint held by the noble framers of our Constitution, I, for one, have ever considered *it* one of

the greatest blessings . . . that God ever bestowed upon a favored nation.[5]

The Effects of the Emancipation Proclamation

The principles of the Emancipation Proclamation helped form the basis for Reconstruction. This was the name given to a huge federal government effort to reshape southern society after the war. Republican leaders created programs in the southern states to protect freedmen and help them obtain education, jobs, and other needed aid. When Reconstruction ended in 1876, however, freedmen lost their newly won rights and power. Former Confederates regained control of state governments, and a long period of discrimination against black Southerners began.

On the national level, the Emancipation Proclamation's effects were much longer lasting. It turned African American voters across the North—and black Southerners who were permitted to vote—into loyal Republicans. This support by black voters helped the Republicans remain the majority political party in the United States until 1932. Only two Democrats were elected president, serving just sixteen of the sixty-eight years. Republicans also controlled both the House and Senate for all but ten years during that period. Not until the nation's next major crisis, the Great Depression of the 1930s, did the Democratic party regain power in the federal government.

The Emancipation Proclamation also played a part in inspiring the civil rights movement of the 1960s. Several years before the hundred-year anniversary of Lincoln's act, the National Association for the Advancement of Colored People, a civil rights organization also known as the NAACP, began to call for "Free by '63." The Emancipation Proclamation's centennial in 1963 marked the progress made during one hundred years of freedom. But it also called attention to the racial inequality that still existed in the United States. In this way, the Emancipation Proclamation helped inspire the huge turnout for the March on Washington that the great black civil rights leader Martin Luther King, Jr., led in August 1963.

The Emancipation Proclamation Today

The official Emancipation Proclamation, copied by hand from the document that Lincoln signed in his study on January 1, 1863, is today held in the National Archives of the United States in Washington, D.C. The document is periodically exhibited. It typically can be seen on the anniversary of its signing or in February as part of Black History Month.

The copy that Lincoln wrote and signed in his study no longer exists. Four photographic copies of it were made. But in late 1863, the president donated the original to a charity in Chicago that was raising money to help Union army troops. It was purchased by a local

Young Texans take part in a modern-day Juneteenth celebration in Austin. Juneteenth is now an official state holiday in Texas.

resident and was later destroyed in the Great Chicago Fire of 1871.

In early 1864, Lincoln also donated the original Preliminary Emancipation Proclamation to help raise money for the U.S. Sanitary Commission, a forerunner of today's Red Cross. In 1865, the New York legislature purchased it for the New York State Library. It remains at the library in Albany today and is occasionally put on public display. The unissued preliminary proclamation that Lincoln first read to his cabinet in July 1862 is in the collections of the Library of Congress in Washington, D.C.

The Emancipation Proclamation continues to be celebrated each year by African Americans throughout the United States. The most common date for these celebrations is June 19.

On June 19, 1865, about a month after the surrender of the last Confederate forces in North Carolina, Union troops landed at Galveston, Texas. They announced that the war was over and that all the slaves were free. A joyous celebration took place. African Americans in Galveston repeated this celebration annually to mark the date of emancipation in Texas. Gradually, these former slaves and their descendants spread across Texas and the United States. For decades, many assembled in Galveston on June 19 each year to celebrate what was called "Juneteenth." Others began similar Juneteenth celebrations in their own communities.

Juneteenth is now observed in every state. It is the oldest known commemoration of the end of slavery. Today Juneteenth draws people of all races to celebrate an event that shaped America's past and continues to influence society. These yearly celebrations assure that Americans do not forget the tremendous contribution Abraham Lincoln and his Emancipation Proclamation made to the nation's history.

★ TIMELINE ★

1619—First Africans in the colonies arrive in Virginia and are treated as indentured servants.

1641—Massachusetts Bay and Plymouth become the first English colonies to legalize slavery.

1663—Maryland law provides that black indentured servants must serve their masters for life.

1682—Virginia enacts a law establishing a distinction between servants and slaves, based on race.

1775—The first American antislavery society is organized in Philadelphia, Pennsylvania; the American Revolution begins.

1776—The Declaration of Independence is issued.

1780—Pennsylvania begins the gradual abolition of slavery, followed by Connecticut and Rhode Island (1784), New York (1785), and New Jersey (1786); Massachusetts ends slavery outright in 1783.

1787—The Northwest Ordinance bans slavery in the Northwest Territory; the legality of slavery is recognized in the nation's new Constitution.

1793—Congress passes the first fugitive slave law, providing for the return of slaves escaping across state lines; Eli Whitney builds the first cotton gin.

1803—The Louisiana Purchase expands the nation's size and the area open to slavery.

1807—Slavery is abolished in Great Britain.

1808—Congress passes a law prohibiting the further importation of slaves into the United States.

1809—Abraham Lincoln is born in Kentucky.

1820—Congress reaches the Missouri Compromise, closing most of the Louisiana Purchase to slavery.

1830—The Lincoln family moves from southern Indiana to Macon County, Illinois.

1833—Great Britain abolishes slavery throughout its empire; the American Anti-Slavery Society is founded.

1834—Abraham Lincoln is elected to the Illinois legislature; he serves until 1841.

1847—Lincoln begins a two-year term in Congress as a representative from Illinois; the antislavery Wilmot Proviso is introduced into Congress.

1854—Congress passes the Kansas-Nebraska Act, which repeals the Missouri Compromise; the Republican party is founded and opposes the spread of slavery.

1856—Lincoln joins the Republican party; fighting erupts in Kansas over the slavery issue.

1858—Lincoln opposes Senator Stephen Douglas for reelection; the Lincoln-Douglas debates occur; Douglas is returned to the Senate.

1860—Lincoln opposes Douglas and two other candidates for president and is elected in November; in December, South Carolina secedes from the United States.

1861—Mississippi, Florida, Alabama, Georgia, Louisiana, and Texas join with South Carolina to form the Confederacy in February; Lincoln becomes president in March; in April and May, Virginia, Arkansas, Tennessee, and North Carolina join the Confederacy; the Civil War begins; in August, Congress acts against slavery by passing the first Confiscation Act.

1862—In July, Congress passes the Militia Act to allow free black men to serve in the army and the Second Confiscation Act to free the South's slaves, and Lincoln writes an emancipation proclamation; in September, following the Union victory at the Battle of Antietam, Lincoln announces the Preliminary Emancipation Proclamation.

1863—The Emancipation Proclamation takes effect on January 1.

1864—Lincoln is reelected president in November.

1865—Confederate general Robert E. Lee surrenders to Union general Ulysses S. Grant on April 9; on April 14, Lincoln is assassinated; in May the remaining Confederate armies surrender and the Civil War ends; in December, the Thirteenth Amendment to the Constitution formally abolishes slavery.

1866—The Fourteenth Amendment makes African Americans citizens.

1870—The Fifteenth Amendment gives African-American men the right to vote.

★ Chapter Notes ★

Chapter 1. Forever Free

1. Roy P. Basler, ed., *The Collected Works of Abraham Lincoln* (New Brunswick, N.J.: Rutgers University Press, 1953), vol. 5, pp. 410, 412, 418.

2. Curt Johnson and Mark McLaughlin, *Civil War Battles* (New York: The Fairfax Press, 1977), p. 67.

3. *The Civil War Society's Encyclopedia of the Civil War* (Princeton, N.J.: Philip Lief Group, Inc., 1997), p. 12.

4. Basler, vol. 5, p. 426.

5. David H. Donald, ed., *Inside Lincoln's Cabinet: The Civil War Diaries of Salmon P. Chase* (New York: Longman's, Green and Company, 1954), p. 150.

6. Basler, vol. 5, p. 434.

7. James McPherson, *Battle Cry of Freedom: The Civil War Era* (New York: Oxford University Press, 1988), p. 558.

8. John Hope Franklin, *The Emancipation Proclamation* (Garden City, N.Y.: Doubleday & Co., 1963), p. 62.

9. Letter to Horace Greeley, August 22, 1862, in Basler, vol. 5, p. 388.

Chapter 2. The Peculiar Institution

1. Betty Wood, *The Origins of American Slavery: Freedom and Bondage in the English Colonies* (New York: Hill and Wang, 1997), p. 78.

2. Ibid., p. 88.

3. *Macmillan Encyclopedia of World Slavery* (New York: Simon & Schuster Macmillan, 1998), p. 865.

4. Eric Foner and John A. Garraty, eds., *The Reader's Companion to American History* (Boston: Houghton Mifflin Company, 1991), p. 992.

5. United States Department of Commerce, Bureau of the Census, *Historical Statistics of the United States* (Washington, D.C.: Government Printing Office, 1976), vol. 1, p. 22; Mabel M. Smythe, *The Black American Reference Book* (Englewood Cliffs, N.J.: Prentice-Hall, Inc., 1976), p. 23; Harold D. Woodman, ed., *Slavery and the Southern Economy* (New York: Harcourt, Brace & World, Inc., 1966), pp. 14–15.

6. Frederick Douglass, *Narrative of the Life of Frederick Douglass* (New York: New American Library, 1968), pp. 73, 75.

7. Kwame Appiah and Henry Louis Gates, Jr., eds., *Africana: The Encyclopedia of the African and African American Experience* (New York: Basic Civitas Books, 1999), pp. 784, 793.

Chapter 3. The Antislavery Crusade

1. Article I, section 9, clause 1 of the Constitution of the United States.

2. Article IV, section 2, clause 3 of the Constitution of the United States.

3. Daniel J. Boorstin, ed., *An American Primer* (New York, NY: New American Library, Inc., 1966), pp. 278–279.

4. "An Address to the Slaves of the United States of America" in Thomas R. Frazier, ed., *Afro-American History: Primary Sources* (New York: Harcourt, Brace & World, Inc., 1970), p. 115.

Chapter 4. The Lone Star of Illinois

1. Michael Burlingame, *The Inner World of Abraham Lincoln* (Urbana: University of Illinois Press, 1994), p. 21.

2. Ibid.

3. Ibid.

4. Ibid., p. 22.

5. *The American Heritage Pictorial History of the Presidents of the United States* (American Heritage Publishing Company, 1968), vol. 1, p. 383.

6. Roy P. Basler, ed., *The Collected Works of Abraham Lincoln* (New Brunswick, N.J.: Rutgers University Press, 1953), vol. 1, p. 75.

7. Ibid., pp. 111, 113.

8. Burlingame, pp. 26–27.

9. David H. Donald, *Lincoln* (New York: Simon & Schuster, 1995), pp. 85–89.

10. Donald, p. 103.

11. Ibid., p. 168.

12. Basler, vol. 2, p. 461.

13. Donald, p. 209.

Chapter 5. Now Is the Time

1. James McPherson, *Ordeal by Fire: The Civil War and Reconstruction* (New York: Alfred A. Knopf, 1982), p. 125.

2. Roy P. Basler, ed., *The Collected Works of Abraham Lincoln* (New Brunswick, N.J.: Rutgers University Press, 1953), vol. 4, p. 139.

3. Ibid., p. 160.

4. Ibid., p. 151.

5. Ibid., p. 263.

6. Ibid., pp. 265, 271.

7. Philip S. Foner, ed., *The Life and Writings of Frederick Douglass* (New York: International Publishers Co., Inc., 1952), vol. 3, pp. 90–91.

8. Basler, vol. 4, p. 506.

9. David H. Donald, *Lincoln* (New York: Simon & Schuster, 1995), p. 315.

10. Frank Donovan, *Mr. Lincoln's Proclamation* (New York: Dodd, Mead & Company, 1964), p. 98.

11. Ibid., p. 100.

12. James McPherson, *Battle Cry of Freedom: The Civil War Era* (New York: Oxford University Press, 1988), p. 495.

13. Basler, vol. 5, p. 48.

14. Donovan, p. 102.

15. Basler, vol. 5, p. 318.

16. Gideon Welles, "The History of Emancipation," *The Galaxy,* vol. 14 (December 1872), pp. 842–843.

17. Basler, vol. 5, p. 329.

18. Ibid., p. 336.

Chapter 6. The Dawn of Freedom

1. Frank Donovan, *Mr. Lincoln's Proclamation* (New York: Dodd, Mead & Company, 1964), p. 109.

2. David H. Donald, *Lincoln* (New York: Simon & Schuster, 1995), p. 370.

3. Roy P. Basler, ed., *The Collected Works of Abraham Lincoln* (New Brunswick, N.J.: Rutgers University Press, 1953), vol. 5, pp. 403–404.

4. Ibid., pp. 419–420, 425.

5. David H. Donald, ed., *Inside Lincoln's Cabinet: The Civil War Diaries of Salmon P. Chase* (New York: Longmans, Green and Co., 1954), p. 150.

6. Donald, *Inside Lincoln's Cabinet,* pp. 150–151.

7. Basler, vol. 5, p. 438.

8. Ibid., p. 434.

9. Ibid.

10. Donald, *Lincoln,* p. 377.

11. John Hope Franklin, *The Emancipation Proclamation* (Garden City, N.Y.: Doubleday & Co., 1963), p. 63.

12. James M. McPherson, *Battle Cry of Freedom* (New York: Oxford University Press, 1988), p. 558.

13. Allan Nevins, *Ordeal of the Union* (New York: Scribner, 1959), vol. 2, p. 239.

14. William C. Davis, *Lincoln's Men: How President Lincoln Became Father to an Army and a Nation* (New York: The Free Press, 1999), p. 94.

15. Basler, vol. 5, p. 434.

16. Franklin, p. 71.

17. Donald, *Lincoln,* p. 377.

18. Ibid., p. 383.

19. Lincoln quoted in Donovan, p. 117; Sumner and Brown quoted in Franklin, p. 90.

20. F. B. Carpenter, *The Inner Life of Abraham Lincoln: Six Months at the White House* (Boston: Houghton, Osgood and Company, 1880), p. 269.

21. Franklin, p. 95.

22. J. G. Randall and David H. Donald, *The Civil War and Reconstruction,* 2nd ed., (Lexington, Mass.: D.C. Heath and Company, 1969), p. 381.

23. Richard A. Long, ed., *Black Writers and the American Civil War* (Secaucus, N.J.: The Blue & Grey Press, 1988), p. 177.

24. Davis, p. 101.

25. Randall and Donald, p. 387.

26. Donald, *Lincoln,* p. 430.

27. Ibid., p. 431.

28. Philip Foner, ed., *The Life and Writings of Frederick Douglass* (New York: International Publishers Co. Inc., 1952), vol. 3, p. 318.

29. Basler, vol. 6, pp. 409–410.

Chapter 7. A Long Way to Go

1. Philip Foner, ed., *The Life and Writings of Frederick Douglass* (New York: International Publishers Co. Inc., 1952), vol. 3, p. 365.

2. Roy P. Basler, ed., *The Collected Works of Abraham Lincoln* (New Brunswick, N.J.: Rutgers University Press, 1953), vol. 7, p. 281.

3. Ibid., vol. 6, pp. 428–429.

4. Richard N. Current, *The Lincoln Nobody Knows* (New York: Hill and Wang, 1958), p. 228.

5. Frank Donovan, *Mr. Lincoln's Proclamation* (New York: Dodd, Mead & Company, 1964), pp. 140–141.

★ FURTHER READING ★

Books

Judson, Karen. *Abraham Lincoln.* Berkeley Heights, N.J.: Enslow Publishers, Inc., 1998.

Macht, Norman L., and Mary Hall. *The History of Slavery.* San Diego, Calif.: Lucent Books, 1997.

Offosu-Appiah, L. H. *People in Bondage: African Slavery Since the 15th Century.* Minneapolis, Minn.: Rhinestone Press, 1993.

Roberts, Russell. *Lincoln and the Abolition of Slavery.* San Diego, Calif.: Greenhaven Press, 2000.

Taylor, Kimberly Hayes. *Black Abolitionists and Freedom Fighters.* Minneapolis, Minn.: The Oliver Press, Inc., 1996.

Internet Addresses

Brix, Rick J. *Abraham Lincoln Biographical Outline.* <http://condor.stcloudstate.edu/~brixr01/ALincolnbiooutline.html>

Franklin, John Hope. *The Emancipation Proclamation: An Act of Justice. April 5, 2001.* <http://www.nara.gov/publications/prologue/franklin.html>

WGBH Educational Foundation and PBS Online. *The Time of the Lincolns.* <http://www.pbs.org/wgbh/amex/lincolns>

★ INDEX ★